The Parables of Judgment

by

Robert Farrar Capon

WILLIAM B. EERDMANS PUBLISHING COMPANY
GRAND RAPIDS, MICHIGAN

Copyright © 1989 by Wm. B. Eerdmans Publishing Co.
255 Jefferson Ave. S.E., Grand Rapids, Mich. 49503

Reprinted, May 1990

Library of Congress Cataloging-in-Publication Data

Capon, Robert Farrar.
The parables of judgment.

1. Jesus Christ—Parables. I. Title.
BT375.2.C325   1988   226′.806   88-33510
ISBN 0-8028-3650-X

Contents

v

The Parables of Judgment

CHAPTER ONE

Introduction

*Inclusion before Exclusion as the Touchstone of the
Parables of Judgment*

The theme of judgment — of
crisis, of decisive, history-altering and history-fulfilling action
on the part of God—is present in Jesus' teaching from the earliest days of his ministry. At first, his pronouncements about
judgment are couched in more or less traditional language: like
the stock apocalyptic scenarios of the later prophets and the
revivalist movements of Jesus' time, their imagery implies that
God will intervene in history at some final day and settle its
score not only with a bang but with plenty of whimpering on
the part of the world. In a word, Jesus starts out sounding like
John the Baptist. But as he develops the theme, this judgment,
this *krísis,* gradually becomes more complex. Simple intervention on God's part is replaced by puzzling images of nonintervention. Direct, right-handed action that rewards the righteous and punishes the wicked is downplayed in favor of a
mysterious, left-handed dispensation that indiscriminately ex-
alts the last, the lost, the least, and the little—a dispensation,
in fact, that achieves its goal by the vast leveling action of a
universal resurrection of the dead. So much so, that when Jesus
finally comes to deliver his formal parables of judgment, he
tells them all in the last few days before the crucifixion. Therefore, if there is a single, major subtext to his developed teaching about judgment—if he has in mind any unifying, govern-

ing principle in these parables — it is sure to be something closely linked to his own death and resurrection.

I say no more at this point about what that subtext might be. The burden of this book will be to discover it—not only by a detailed examination of Jesus' parables of judgment as they appear in the Gospels of Matthew, Mark, and Luke but also by a comparison of those parables with other judgment passages from the Gospel of John to Revelation. Naturally (since the synoptic Gospels sometimes differ in their sequences of events and parables), this will require a harmonizing of the biblical accounts into a single order. I shall not, however, foist on you a harmony of my own; instead, I shall adopt the numbering system for Gospel passages devised by Kurt Aland in the Greek-English edition of the *Synopsis Quattuor Evangeliorum* (United Bible Societies).* Beyond that, only a few housekeeping details need mentioning here. I shall be working from the original Greek — principally from the text employed by Aland in the *Synopsis,* but also from the second edition of the Aland, Black, Martini, Metzger, Wikgren text, from the twenty-second edition of the Nestle text, and from the Schmoller Concordance to the Nestle text. The translations offered will be largely my own, but they will take into account the versions I habitually consult: the King James Version (KJV), the Revised Standard Version (RSV), Today's English Version (TEV), the New International Version (NIV), and, to a lesser degree, the Clementine Vulgate (VgCL), the Jerusalem Bible (JB), the New English Bible (NEB), and the New Testament in Modern English by J. B. Phillips (JBP).

Let us begin, then. We have three sources for assessing the note of judgment in Jesus' early teaching, all of them to be found on the pages of the synoptic Gospels. They are: the Jewish establishment of his time (most commonly instanced

---

*An English edition of *Synopsis of the Four Gospels* is available from the American Bible Society for $8.95. It is the ideal companion to this book for study purposes.

by the Gospel writers as the Pharisees, the scribes, or the Herodians); the disciples and/or the apostles; and, of course, Jesus himself. I take them up in that order.

There is no question that, almost from the first, the religious authorities of the day perceived Jesus' words and deeds as a judgment of their trusteeship of the revelation of God. It never seems to have occurred to them to write him off as a maverick. They automatically assumed he was a danger and, as early as Mark 3:6, they were canvassing the possibility of destroying him. From our point of view, of course, the scribes and Pharisees are almost characters in a hiss-and-boo melodrama: the moustache-twirling, cloak-and-dagger parts that the Gospel writers assign them seem overwrought. But from their own point of view, they were quite correct. Powers that be are always expert sniffers of the wind and testers of the waters. They can spot a threat to their system a mile off: all they need is half a sentence from a professor or the odd gesture from a political figure and their heresy-alarm goes off like a klaxon. And Jesus provided them with far more cause for alarm than that. The common people may have been "astonished at his teaching because he taught them as one who had authority *(exousía)* and not as the scribes" (Mark 1:22). And the crowds may have been captivated by his healings and titillated by his consorting with publicans and sinners. But the experts knew better: he was, pure and simple, a menace. Not only was he shaking the foundations of the Torah; he was also certain to make political trouble and bring down the wrath of Rome on their heads. In other words, he threatened to precipitate a judgment they were unable to see as the work of God—to bring about the crisis that would put an end not only to their stewardship of the divine dispensation but also, as they saw it, to the dispensation itself.

The disciples, by contrast, displayed a less critical but still keen perception of the judgmental aspect of Jesus' ministry. For the most part, they were ordinary people, with ordinary people's enthusiasm for anything that promises to even scores and administer comedowns to the mighty. They were, if you will, downright eschatology buffs: they positively itched to hear the note of judgment, and they supplied it full force even in contexts where Jesus barely mentioned it. When I expounded the parable of the Wheat and the Weeds in my previous book, *The Parables of the Kingdom,* * I took the view that Jesus' ham-fisted, judgment-loaded allegorization of the parable (Matt. 13:36-43) was not so much a considered expression of his own ideas on the subject as it was a sop thrown to their inordinate fondness for hellfire and brimstone. Indeed, so enamored were they of their own rockem-sockem, right-handed notions of divine crisis management that Jesus had a hard time getting through to them his essentially left-handed, noninterventionist view of the authentic judgment of God. Three times, for example, he predicted his coming death and resurrection (in Matt. 16; 17; and 20—see also the parallel passages in Mark and Luke). But even though he did so in plain Aramaic, with not a smitch of parabolic obfuscation— and even though those predictions bore witness to his conviction that judgment operates more by God's going out of the judging business than by staying in it—they never moved an inch beyond their conviction that judgment simply had to work by retribution, and in their time at that. In fact, their expectation of direct intervention was so strong that even at the point of Jesus' ascension (Acts 1:6), they still felt compelled to ask him whether he would *now* finally cut out the indirection and get on with some intelligible tidying up of history.

And subsequent generations of disciples have not done much better than they did, even though we have had the rest of the New Testament and two thousand years of reflection to lend us a hand. The church, by and large, has always been more receptive to judgment-as-settling-scores than to judgment as proceeding out of, and in accordance with, the reconciling grace of resurrection. Christian preachers regularly blow the Gospel of grace clean out of the water with sermons that make

---

The Parables of the Kingdom (Grand Rapids: Zondervan, 1985), pp. 123-131.

reward and punishment, not resurrection with its sovereign pardon, the touchstone of judgment. And Christians generally —every day of the week and twice on Sundays in some cases —hear them gladly. The church has found that plain old hanging-judge sermons sell, but that grace remains a drug on the market. As a preacher, I can with the greatest of ease tell people that God is going to get them, and I can be sure they will believe every word I say. But what I cannot do, without inviting utter disbelief and serious doubts about my sanity, is proclaim that he has in fact taken away *all* the sins of the world and that he has, accordingly, solved all the problems he once had with sin. I cannot tell them, as John does, that he "did not come to judge the world but to save the world" (John 12:47). Nor can I ask them, as Paul does, to believe the logical consequence of that statement, namely, that "there is therefore now no condemnation to those who are in Christ Jesus" (Rom. 8:1). Because if I do, the same old questions will come pouring out: "What about Hitler?" "What about child molesters?" "What about my skunk of a brother-in-law?" Their one pressing worry is always, "What have you done with the hell we know and love?"

But that gets us ahead of the story; it is time to turn to the third and most considerable source we have for assessing the nature of judgment in the Gospels: Jesus himself.

The usual view is that Jesus' early teaching about the subject is traditional—that he started out, as I have said, sounding like John the Baptist and identifying himself with customary apocalyptic notions of a forcible and fiery settling of the world's hash. But even at the beginning, his teaching was more complex than that. In his first telling of the parable of the Wheat and the Weeds (Matt. 13:24-30), for example, he spends almost all of his time (verses 24-30a) indicating that God's way of dealing with sin is by forbearance—by an *áphesis,* a forgiveness of evil, a letting-be of the badness of the world, even a permission of sin. Only in verse 30b does he introduce the image of the harvest *(therismós)* at which the weeds will be separated from the wheat and burned in the fire. True enough, in the interpretation of the parable he does speak (Matt. 13:40) in traditional terms of the judgment as the end, the wrap-up of the age *(hē synteleía tou aiōnos)*. But elsewhere in the synoptic Gospels as well as in the rest of the New Testament other words come to the fore. John habitually uses the word *krísis* (judgment) and its verb *krínein* (to judge) when Jesus speaks on the subject; Paul commonly uses another variant of the same root, *kríma* (judgment, condemnation), to express his own views. As a matter of fact, it will be precisely to those usages that I shall look for the fully developed scriptural notion of judgment. In the next chapter, I shall try to explicate their significance. Here, let me just continue working from the Gospels: even in them there is an evident development of the left-handed view of judgment.

Consider the passage toward which not only the synoptics but also the Gospel of John build: the passion narrative. It is impossible to make too much of its presence as the climactic portion of all four books. The sheer, disproportionate length of the accounts of Jesus' trial and death argues conclusively for their paramount importance in the Gospel writers' minds. The events themselves occupied less than twenty-four hours of Jesus' life (from Maundy Thursday night to three o'clock on Good Friday afternoon); yet they are given an inordinate amount of space in the Gospels. For the record, the figures are: in Matthew, two chapters out of twenty-eight; in Mark, two chapters out of sixteen; in Luke, two chapters out of twenty-four; and in John, seven chapters out of twenty-one. To me, that says plainly that there is no way of leaving what Jesus actually did as the final act of his ministry out of our assessment of what he thought and taught about the ultimate action of God in judgment. It says that the *krísis*, the judgment, is precisely one of forgiveness, of a saving grace that works by death and resurrection. For at the consummate moment of God's mysterious intervention in history, he operates by nonintervention—by a hands-off rather than a hands-on policy. On the cross, with nails through his hands and feet, he does all that he judges needs doing; and he does it all by doing precisely nothing. He just dies. He does not get mad. He does not get even. He just gets out.

For me, nothing else holds a candle to that. The words of Jesus on the subject of judgment may be debatable (though I hope to show in this book that they are not nearly as debatable as some think). But the action of Jesus in his passion — his saving, judging *inaction,* if you will—governs everything. And not just for us who sit here in the community of faith with twenty centuries' worth of theology to guide (or confuse) us. Jesus himself made the crucifixion/resurrection the governing center of his developed teaching. From the feeding of the five thousand onward (that is, beginning at Matt. 14; Mark 6; Luke 9; and John 6), death is uppermost in his mind. Not only does he predict his own death three times after that point, and not only does he undertake his final journey to Jerusalem (Luke 9–18) specifically as a going to the cross; to clinch the case, he makes death (and its cognates, lastness, lostness, least-ness, and littleness) the touchstone of all of his parables during that journey. (I have dealt with those parables at length in my previous volume, *The Parables of Grace;* there is neither space nor need to say more about them here.)*

In any case, it is the imminence of Jesus' passion and death that gives his parables of judgment their singular force and supplies them with their most profound interpretative principles. Fascinatingly, the most memorable of them occur on the four days between Palm Sunday and Good Friday; and all the rest of them are to be found just prior to that time. This juxtaposition means first of all that the parables of judgment are hot, not cool. They are paradoxical stories told by a Savior on his way to a dreadful yet fully chosen death; they are not eschatological chitchat dispensed by a theology professor sauntering to a lecture. A death sentence, as Doctor Johnson noted, focuses the mind mightily. The fairest and most natural reading of all these parables, therefore, will always be one that makes death and resurrection the principal clue to what

---

The Parables of Grace (Grand Rapids: Eerdmans, 1988).

Jesus is talking about. It is a mistake to come at them as if we already understood what judgment is all about and were simply trying to see how they can be made to confirm what we think. Come at them that way and you will get only what so many preachers have gotten: a Messiah playing cops and robbers, a vindictive God bent on putting all the baddies under flat rocks. But come to them as the words of a Savior who has just spent weeks or months making death the principal device of his parables of gracious love—and who is now, under the compulsion of the same gracious love, about to die in order to activate the device once and for all—and you will see something new. You will see Gospel, not law; good news, not bad; vindication, not vindictiveness.

At the beginning of my study of Jesus' parables I divided them into three groups: the parables of the kingdom, which run from the start of his ministry to the feeding of the five thousand; the parables of grace, which run from the feeding of the five thousand to Palm Sunday; and the parables of judgment, which are compressed for the most part into Holy Week. I want to add a note to that division now. If I were asked to assign a *color* to each of the three groups, I would call the parables of the kingdom green, the parables of grace purple, and the parables of judgment white. Consider.

The kingdom parables are green because so many of them are about growing—about seeds and plants. They are about the mystery of a kingdom already planted, a kingdom at hand, a kingdom in our midst—a kingdom, above all, that grows and prevails as a seed does: by its own sovereign power and not by any efforts of ours. In the parable of the Sower, for example (Mark 4:1-9), the seed sown succeeds in doing its proper thing despite the circumstances: what falls by the road successfully attracts birds; what falls on the shallow or the thorny ground grows as best it can; and what falls on the good ground bears fruit on the basis of its own peculiar power, some thirty-, some sixty-, some a hundredfold. Or take the Seed Cast by the Farmer on his Field (Mark 4:26-29): the man lies down and gets up night and day, but the seed sprouts and grows "he knows not how"—from an earth that "bears fruit of itself," quite apart from his instrumentality. Or, finally, take the Yeast (Matt. 13:33): the woman puts it into three measures of flour at the very creation of the lump of dough and the yeast grows until the whole is leavened. Let us make green, then, the color of these early parables of the mysterious, already present, catholic kingdom of God.

Purple, though, for the parables of grace. Purple, because they are about passionate, selfless love (the Good Samaritan, the Prodigal Son); but purple above all because they are about a love that works by death. "Greater love has no one than this," Jesus said, "that he lay down his life for his friends" (John 15:13). Death is the mainspring of the parables of grace. For example, the Prodigal Son (Luke 15:11-32) is practically a festival of death: the father dies at the beginning of the parable by putting his will into effect; the prodigal dies in the far country when his life as he knew it comes to an end in bitter poverty; the prodigal dies again—fruitfully, this time—when he comes home, confesses that he is a dead son, and wisely leaves out of his confession the irrelevant, life-protracting request that he be taken back as a hired hand; finally, the fatted calf dies to make possible the party that is the point of the whole parable. Or consider the Lost Sheep (Luke 15:1-7): a lost sheep wandering in the wilderness is, for all intents and purposes, a dead sheep; ninety-nine abandoned sheep are, for the period of the shepherd's absence at least, likewise in danger of death; and a shepherd who puts all of his efforts into a search for a single lost sheep virtually dies to the sheep-ranching business, exposing himself to the loss of *all* his sheep. Moreover, even the parables of grace that do not directly express this theme of love operating by death still embody it: they are, all of them, spoken by a Savior consciously on his way to die for love. Death, therefore—and in particular, death as the fountainhead of grace—is what colors these parables purple.

The parables of judgment, however, are white. I said that they were hot, not cool; and of all the colors that can represent heat, white is the hottest. Red-hot passion scarcely rises above the level of sexual excitement; white-hot passion is love to the ultimate degree. More than that, white is the color of light; in John's Gospel it is precisely the light of the world, Jesus himself, who brings on the judgment—who provokes the *krísis* of the world. Jesus says, "This is the judgment, that light has come into the world, and people loved the darkness rather than the light because their deeds were evil." But above all, the parables of judgment are white because, like white light, they contain all the colors of the other parables and will, if refracted through the prism of a sound interpretation, manifest them with perfect clarity.

If I have anything to contribute to the interpretation of the parables of judgment, it is my steadfast refusal to separate them from the rest of Jesus' parables. I find in them, again and again, not only the green, growing, mysterious, catholic kingdom but also the purple, passionate grace that saves by death. Therefore I am convinced that anyone who interprets them as if Jesus had decided simply to abandon his previous palette—who takes the view, in other words, that Jesus had gotten over his penchant for painting kindly kingdoms and gracious loves and was now getting down to depicting the grim "final solution" in which God gets even with sinners by marching them into the gas chambers of an eternal Dachau—is making a crashing mistake. The Gospel of grace must not be turned into a bait-and-switch offer. It is not one of those airline supersavers in which you read of a $59.00 fare to Orlando only to find, when you try to buy a ticket, that the six seats per flight at that price are all taken and that the trip will now cost you $199.95. Jesus must not be read as having baited us with grace only to clobber us in the end with law. For as the death and resurrection of Jesus were accomplished once and for all, so the grace that reigns by those mysteries reigns eternally—even in the thick of judgment.

Accordingly, while I am playing my cards face up, let me give you what I consider to be the master key to the parables of judgment. As growth-in-a-mystery was the governing device in the parables of the kingdom, and as death-resurrection was the governing device of the parables of grace, so *inclusion before exclusion* is the chief interpretative principle of the parables of judgment. As a general rule — and especially in his specific parables of judgment—Jesus is at pains to show that *no one is kicked out who wasn't already in*. The corroboration of that principle, of course, will be the burden of this entire book; but just to whet your appetite for the labor of exposition, let me give you a few instances of how it manifests itself.

In the parable of the King's Son's Wedding (Matt. 22:1-14), the guest who was cast into outer darkness for not having on a wedding garment was already, by the very terms of the parable — by the host's insistence on dragging in everybody and his brother—a member of the wedding: he was booted out only after he had been invited in. Likewise, in the parable of the Ten Virgins (Matt. 25:1-13), the five foolish girls were every bit as much a part of the wedding reception as the five wise ones; the distinction between the two groups is based on what the wise or the foolish did in response to their already granted acceptance, not on anything they did to earn it. Similarly, in the parable of the Talents (Matt. 25:14-30), all three servants—the one who received a single talent as well as the ones who received two and five—were already in their master's favor. He had laid down his possessions, his whole living; he had died, as it were, for all of them by giving up control over his life. The unfavorable judgment finally pronounced on the one who hid his talent in the ground was based not on whether he was good enough to "earn grace" (a contradiction in terms, please note) but solely on what he did in response to the grace already granted.

But enough specifics for now. I propose to show that judgment, as it is portrayed in the parables of Jesus (not to mention the rest of the New Testament), never comes until *after* acceptance: grace remains forever the sovereign consideration. The difference between the blessed and the cursed is one thing and one thing only: the blessed accept their acceptance and the cursed reject it; but the acceptance is *already in place* for both groups before either does anything about it. To put it another way, heaven is populated by nothing but forgiven sinners and hell is populated by nothing but forgiven sinners: the Lamb of God takes away the sin of the *kósmos,* not just of the chosen few (John 1:29); Jesus said, "I, if I be lifted up, will draw *all* to me" (John 12:32). The difference between heaven and hell, accordingly, is simply that those in heaven accept the endless forgiveness, while those in hell reject it. Indeed, the precise hell of hell is its endless refusal to open the door to the reconciled and reconciling party that stands forever on its porch and knocks, equally endlessly, for permission to bring in the Supper of the Lamb (Rev. 3:20).

But as I said, enough. Time to turn to some of the broader New Testament background of judgment before taking up Jesus' parables themselves.

CHAPTER TWO

The Sovereign Light

Jesus as the Uncondemning Judge

In this chapter, I am going to do three things that in certain circles are considered suspect. I shall quite seriously use the Gospel of John as a source for Jesus' teaching about judgment; I shall expound that teaching by arguing from some words attributed to Jesus in the book of Revelation; and most alarmingly of all, I shall maintain that the usual distinction between the historical Jesus and the Christ of faith (a distinction that almost always ends up boosting the former and knocking the latter) is historically inaccurate, scripturally pointless, and fundamentally mischievous.

Since it promises to be the most fun, let me undertake the last project first. The practice of giving the "simple Jesus" of the synoptic Gospels primacy over the "complex Christ" of, say, Paul or John—of saying, in effect, that it is the church, and not the Jesus of history, that is the source of what finally became the Christian view of judgment—is a fast shuffle followed by a misplayed card. To begin with, it dates mostly from the nineteenth century, a period whose most publicized theological fracas was the war between science and religion. This conflict, which in some quarters is still thought to be raging full force, was misapprehended, misguided, and misreported from the start. Except in the minds of partisans and publicists, it should never have been fought at all.

On the secular side, it was provoked by philosophico-

15

theological extrapolations from certain scientific "discoveries"—among them the then new findings of paleontology and comparative biology—and it was fueled by a philosophical theory of upward evolutionary progress that had been gaining acceptance since the end of the eighteenth century. The notion that creation was developing and improving quite on its own had been around for some time before Darwin. Evolutionism was not cooked up as a necessary conclusion of Darwin's work; his work, rather, came to be seen as a serendipitous proof that the already popular doctrine of evolutionary progress had some basis in fact. But this in turn produced a standoff. On the one hand, the partisans of the secular view decided that the biblical accounts of creation simply had to be wrong; on the other hand, the defenders of the faith went to the opposite extreme and maintained that the Scriptures were correct in every detail.

Both sides were mistaken. The "scientific" position in no way necessitated positing the absence of God: philosophically speaking (and this was precisely a philosophical war, not a religio-scientific one), God could just as well have presided over an evolving creation as over an instantaneous one. Nor was the religionists' position any better: their taking refuge in the notion that the Scriptures were literally true in every respect would have come as a shock to almost all pre-nineteenth-century Christians—to Paul, for example, or to Augustine, or to Aquinas, or to Luther—all of whom assigned to Scripture far more senses than just the literal one. Neither side, in short, was above making strategic blunders.

But coupled with this mistaken joining of battle on the field of evolution was a philosophical false start: a deistic notion of God that had been around even longer than evolutionism and that had infected the troops of God's champions as well as those of his enemies. Deism—the doctrine that says that God made a perfectly adequate, self-managing world and that, on principle, he does not ever obtrude himself upon it by special interventions (miracles, for example) — had been around for a good part of the eighteenth century. When the nineteenth century opened, there were more than a few religionists who were quite ready to cave in to the secularists' objection to the miraculous. By the time the twentieth century began, their numbers were vastly increased: throughout the Christian intellectual community there was a strong bias against anything that even vaguely resembled a divine finger in the pie.

That bias, however, tricked the Christian strategists into fighting the war between science and religion with their opponents' weapon, namely, a deistic God who didn't interfere in the history of the world. In the hands of the secularists, of course, that weapon was a natural one; but in the hands of Christians it was an odd gun indeed. Not only were the Scriptures embarrassingly well stocked with miraculous interventions; the very notion of a revelation that worked ultimately by incarnation should have made them suspect they were shooting with a rifle that might blow up in their faces. But they didn't; and as a result, the whole course of biblical criticism was altered by their reliance on the faulty weapon of deism.

For in order to wage an intellectually respectable war, they simply assumed (fundamentalists excepted, of course) that their only hope of winning lay in downplaying the familiar, theologized Christ of Paul and John in favor of a hitherto unrecognized "historical" Jesus whom they then proceeded to discover, not to say invent. This "quest for the historical Jesus" (the phrase itself is an example of publicists' hype: the original title of Schweitzer's landmark book was *Von Reimarus zu Wrede*) has been a millstone around the neck of biblical criticism ever since. Not that the quest was all bad: what Jesus might actually have thought in his first-century, Jewish mind is by no means irrelevant; it deserves, in fact, all the attention we can give it. But to act as if it is the only legitimate base for Christian biblical study is to overlook some crucial facts.

For one thing, the sources we have for determining the mind of the historical Jesus generally postdate the sources we have for the Christ of faith. In the words of a memorable tag line, "the Gospels were written for the sake of the epistles." Consider. The authentic Pauline corpus was completed before Paul's death in A.D. 64; Mark may have existed in its present form before then, but Matthew, Luke, and John are, by common agreement, later productions. That alone should have given critics pause. It means that the early church got its hands on the so-called simple Jesus of the Gospels only *after* it had been living comfortably with the complex Christ of Paul. But it also means that, without any serious evidence of disgruntlement with the eventually canonical Gospels, the church *perceived no discrepancy between those two purported brands of Savior.* At the very least therefore, the nineteenth- and twentieth-century penchant for opposing a "historical" construct of Jesus to the wider scriptural view of him that in historic fact appeared first—for setting Matthew and Luke, say, against Paul—should be suspect.

But for another thing, it must be remembered that we have the four Gospels we now accept only because the early church, for its own sufficient reasons, winnowed them out from among others and chose to pass them on to us. On any sane view of the inspiration of Scripture, the Holy Spirit did not preside over its composition simply by chloroforming its several authors and then guiding their ballpoint pens into automatically writing what he wanted to say. His presidency over the process of forming Scripture involved not only authors in all their conscious individuality and peculiarity; it also involved, in an equally conscious way, their audience. In the last analysis, as a matter of fact, it was *the community of faith*—the early church—that he used to decide which books were, and which were not, to be considered Scripture.

I say all this (which possibly may not have been as much fun for you as I promised) because the history of biblical criticism in the twentieth century has been a long, painful, and not wholly conclusive struggle to rid itself of the nineteenth century's unfortunate disregard of the early church's role in determining who and what Jesus might be. We have come a good way beyond all that by now, of course; yet the legacy of the false opposition between science and religion—and in particular of the deistic prejudice against untoward manifestations of divine activity—still persists. We have even managed, in certain circles, to concede the pivotal role of the primitive Christian community and still, because of our undiscarded prejudices, turn it against the very faith that led that community to hand us the Gospels to begin with.

To this day, it is a commonplace of much biblical criticism to assume that Jesus of Nazareth could not possibly have done or thought many of the things the Gospels quite plainly assign to him. We are told, for example, that he never meant (or even said — his words are taken as "second-century ecclesiastical glosses") that he was the Messiah, or the Son of man. Or, to take a different example of the same tendency, we are told that while his death may be a thoroughly creditable proposition, his resurrection and ascension must be viewed as the fabricated trappings of a nonhistorical "Christ-event" assignable only to the realm of faith—as if, that is, they were on the pages of Scripture not because they actually happened but because the early church concocted the "happenings" in order to give concrete expression to otherwise uncorroborated beliefs.

Such assertions, of course, cannot be proved or disproved; but they can certainly be shown to be suspicious. They proceed not out of scriptural evidence but out of the still present, and to this day still unexamined, deistic prejudice against miracles. To be sure, the resurrection and the ascension are not *simply* miraculous events. They are not just divine irruptions into an otherwise unchanged order; rather they are manifestations — sacraments, real presences — of a mysterious new creation that was, equally mysteriously, present from the foundation of the world. But for all that, it is totally unnecessary to deny that they were *real* presences — *physical* sacraments, *actual* occurrences — unless, of course, you happen to be a deist. For who else, other than a deist, would think it necessary to assign the risen Lord's sailing up into the clouds to Luke's fertile mind rather than to Jesus' decision literally to do so? Why give Luke the credit for *think-*

ing up the acted parable of the ascension, yet refuse Jesus credit for *acting it out*? Only because you have an a priori principle that Jesus couldn't or wouldn't have done such a thing. But that principle, please note, is based entirely on philosophical prejudice and not at all on scriptural warrant.

I say all this partly to distance myself from what I take to be a mistaken sort of biblical criticism but mostly to alert you to the fact that you must not expect me to be a biblical critic's biblical critic at all. I am a theologian by trade, not a biblical scholar; long ago (for the historical reasons I have already adduced in this chapter), I despaired of the kind of biblical study in which I, along with so many others, was trained. I bring to this exposition of Jesus' parables of judgment a theologian's free-ranging regard for the whole of Scripture, not a critic's narrow attention to what might have been the content of Jesus' teaching only. And I do that because, as I said, we would never have had Jesus' teaching to begin with if it had not been for the church that the Holy Spirit used to give us the rest of the New Testament's teaching about Jesus. I will not set the one against the other. I insist on seeing them as of a piece, and I will not explain or apologize for that insistence any further.

Except to alert you to one more fact you should bear in mind. All trades have their blind spots: if the biblical-criticism fraternity has, for a good century now, suffered from a form of tunnel vision that prevented it from seeing philosophical errors out of the corner of its eye, the theologians' union has, for a lot longer than that, had an inordinate fondness for system. By the very nature of their craft, theologians are dedicated to making things philosophically tidy. If you want (as who doesn't?) a neat synthesis in which all the diverse pieces of revelation are gracefully tied together with a single ribbon of coherent principle, then they are the people to send for. But you must watch them like a hawk, because they can twist almost any two facts, however incompatible, into a thread—and with that thread, they can weave wonderfully. Fair warning then. Even if I am good, I am no better than the rest of my fellow workers on the theological loom. Always feel the goods: it's you, after all, who have to wear the suit.

To work, therefore. Let me try to make clear my thoughts on judgment by noting the way in which the Greek words for judgment are used in the New Testament. Take *kríma* (judgment, condemnation) first. While the word is used in a few places in the Gospels and elsewhere, the passage that unquestionably contains its most difficult and pregnant uses lies in chapters 2 and 3 of Paul's Epistle to the Romans. The difficulties, by and large, stem from a peculiarity in the way Paul wrote his epistles; the pregnancy of meaning, though, derives from the very heart of his thinking.

With no biblical writer more than Paul is it necessary to bear in mind where his argument is going; it is never enough simply to take what he says before he reaches that point and run with it as if it were his final word on the subject at hand. He dictated his letters. He worked, that is, from notes, proceeding through his argument more as an orator on a podium than as a writer at his desk. That means that he had both the freedom and the drawbacks of a speaker. He was free to expand at length on points that were incidental to the progress of his argument; but by the same token, he often expanded at such length that he said things which, taken out of the overall context, can seem to run counter to the argument itself.

Two examples will suffice. For the first, consider what presumably was contained in Paul's dictation notes for 1 Cor. 1. The items might well have been as follows: (1) Open with general greeting. (2) Thank God for the Corinthian church. (3) Warn them against partisan tendencies. (4) Begin main point about Foolishness and Weakness of God. He got through points (1) and (2) nicely; but when he got to point (3), he bogged down. In the course of warning the Corinthians not to say things like "I belong to Paul's party," or "I belong to Apollos," or "I belong to Cephas," he dropped the remark, "Thank God I didn't baptize any of you. . . ." His intention, of course, was simply to say, ". . . otherwise, you'd probably just use that as an excuse for more partisanship." But he immediately remembered that he had indeed baptized Crispus and Gaius; and in the next breath he remembered baptizing the entire family of Stephanus. So, since he was dictating this letter—speaking it rather than writing it—he had to make his corrections as a speaker rather than as a writer. He could not just erase his words or move the cursor back and zap them out; he had to add his corrections as he went along and then get out of his unfortunate digression with a resounding, "But let's get off that subject and on to the main point." Which is exactly what he did. After weasling out of the question of how many people he actually baptized with "I just don't remember if I baptized anyone else" (1 Cor. 1:16), he began verse 17 with "But Christ didn't send me to baptize but to preach the Gospel"—and leapt decisively to point (4), the Power of Christ crucified.

You see the danger, of course. Paul was wandering down a byroad. An unwary interpreter could easily try to make a large point of his baptismal activities; but that would be a false start because it had only a tangential connection with what he actually set out to say. Thus my second example of Pauline digression: chapters 9–11 of Romans. Paul had begun chapter 8 with the glorious statement that "There is therefore now no condemnation (*katákrima*) to those who are in Christ Jesus"; and he ended it with the even more glorious assertion that "nothing can separate us from the love of God in Christ Jesus our Lord." This is the climax of his argument thus far, and his notes now tell him that, after dealing for a bit with the relationship of Israel to all this grace and mercy, he is to make the point (which he finally gets to in Rom. 11:26ff.) that "all Israel will be saved." But on the way to that point, he talks himself into one of the most memorable (and for the unwary interpreter, disastrous) detours in the whole of Scripture. All of the raw materials for double predestination—for God's right to condemn whoever he damn well pleases—come pouring out of him: the pot that can't speak back to the potter, the potter who is free to make vases or chamberpots, and so on. The dreadful doctrine of divine reprobation, therefore, is based on a misreading—not, admittedly, of Paul's actual words, for he did indeed say all those hard things, but *of the force of his words in the context of his whole argument.*

I introduce those examples because the same kind of theological detour is to be found in his uses of *kríma* (and of the verb *krínein*) in chapters 2 and 3 of Romans. In chapter 1 of that epistle, he has spoken of the power of the Good News; he has set down the general principle of justification by faith alone; and he has established the general guilt of all mankind, Jew and Greek alike, before God. He has, in other words, headed himself for chapter 3, in which he will say clearly that *no one* is righteous—that *no one* keeps the law—and that, when righteousness does come to the world, it will not come by the law but will be a gift from God through faith in Jesus Christ. On his way to that conclusion, however, he spends an inordinate amount of time talking about the *kríma tou theoú,* the judgment, the condemnation of God, that rests upon all human beings. Once again, the unwary interpreter is tempted to misread him. The difficult notion of a judgment that regards only the righteousness of Christ enjoyed by faith (a notion, admittedly, that will not receive its definitive statement until Rom. 8) slips away from the reader and only old-style, reward-and-punishment judgment seems to be on Paul's lips. Nevertheless, Rom. 2:1–3:8 remain essentially a detour. They are a parenthesis within his argument, not the main point of it. That comes only when he reaches Rom. 3:9ff., and in particular, 3:22-24: "For there is no difference [no difference, that is, that can be seen as proceeding out of old-line, tit-for-tat *kríma*]; for all have sinned and fallen short of the glory of God, but they are all justified by his grace through the liberating action of Christ Jesus." And Paul then continues in the same, gracious vein: this liberating action is effective for all because God has appointed Jesus a propitiation *(hilastérion)* through faith in his blood in order that God might show his own righteousness *(dikaiosýnēs)* by the forgiveness *(páresin)* of past sins through his forbearance *(anochḗ*—in order, that is, to manifest his righteousness right now *(en tǫ nyn kairǫ,* in the present time) and to prove not only that he himself is righteous *(díkaios)* but that he makes righteous *(dikaioúnta)* those who have faith in Jesus (Rom. 3:25-26).

Romans 2-3, therefore, must be read as an argument in progress. And because the argument does not reach its conclusion until late in chapter 3, it is a mistake to start making conclusions about judgment *(kríma)* in chapter 2. True enough, as you read your way through the passage, your customary view of judgment as God's way of getting even with sinners will tempt you to decide that Paul is coming down hard on the side of that view. But on any fair reading of the entire section you will see that, at the most, he is simply setting you up for a deliverance from that view by means of his favorite subject, grace *(cháris)*—a subject that, for him, remains sovereign over anything you might have thought he was saying about *kríma*.

Admittedly, it takes a bit of doing (perhaps even of fine slicing) to see that. Nevertheless, the fact remains that Paul's view of judgment proceeds *out of* his notion of grace, not *contrary to it*. It is far less difficult, however, to see this radically non-judgmental character of judgment when you come to Jesus' words about *krísis* (judgment) as they appear in the Gospel of John. I give only a single example: the passage that appears in chapter 3 at the end of Jesus' dialogue with Nicodemus, the Pharisee who came to him by night.

Everyone knows and loves John 3:16: "For God so *(hoútos,* thus) loved the world that he gave his only Son that everyone who believes *(pas ho pisteúōn)* in him should not perish but have eternal life." To be sure, that verse alone establishes the primacy of faith *(pístis)* over any rewardable or punishable works; but the rest of the passage (John 3:17-21) expands upon the theme mightily and deserves far more attention than it gets. Let me comment on its verses in order.

Verse 17. "For God did not send his Son into the world that he might judge *(krínē)* the world, but that the world might be saved *(sōthȩ̄)* through him." Jesus repeats the substance of these words in John 12:47, and they are perhaps his most definitive statement on the subject of judgment. To me, they indicate that contrary to all our guilty expectations, God is not mad at the world. Even when he sends his Son to it—the same Son, incidentally, whom he has appointed to do all his judging for him (John 5:22: "the Father judges no one, but has given over all judgment to the Son")—this Son, strangely, does not judge, but rather saves. Not only in this verse, therefore, but throughout the Gospel of John, there lurks the image of the rigged trial, of a judgment at which the judge is shamelessly in cahoots with the guilty world and utterly determined to acquit it no matter what.

Verse 18. "He who believes *(ho pisteúōn)* in him is not judged *(ou krínetai);* but he who does not believe *(ho mē pisteúōn)* has already been judged *(ḗdē kékritai)* because he has not believed *(pepísteuken)* in the name of the only Son of God." All that the world has to do to escape judgment is *believe*—for the simple reason that, by the gracious work of Jesus, it has in fact *already escaped* it. It need do nothing to earn that escape, and it certainly need not compile questionable lists of good works to prove that it deserves to escape. It need not negotiate with God, or be afraid of God, or try conning God into being lenient. It has only to believe that God in Jesus has settled all his problems of sin and to laugh loud and long at how graciously easy the whole business always was. But for those who do not believe—who will not trust the gracious order of the universe revealed in Jesus, who go on insisting on responsibility and accountability and all the other dreadful, losing subjects with which the world beats itself over the head—for them, there is deep trouble. For they have been judged and condemned already by the very fact of their refusal to believe in the nonjudgment already pronounced—in the noncondemnation under which they actually stand—all of which, but for their estranged, stubborn faces, they could be enjoying free of charge.

Verse 19. "And this is the judgment *(krísis):* that the light has come into the world and people loved the darkness rather than the light because their deeds were evil." Yes, Jesus says;

there is indeed a judgment, and that judgment still stands because the law and the prophets I came to fulfill still stand. There is a judgment because the law remains forever your beauty, and when I come to you in my fulfillment of all its righteous demands, I will only make the ugliness of your disobedience look a thousand times worse. But *I* do not judge you. You judge yourself by taking your stand on the law's demands rather than on my righteousness which is yours for the believing. *I* do not condemn you. The law does; but I have lifted the curse of the law and given you a yoke that is easy and a burden that is light: all you need is simply to trust my word that I do not in fact condemn. But if you insist on running from the light of that word into the darkness of your own guilt—if you will not come to me and let me transform your ugliness into my beauty, if you fear my beauty because you dread its contrast with your ugliness—well, then, I cannot help you. Or, better said, you cannot receive the help I have already delivered to you because you choose not to trust my assurance that you already have it. I wish we could do business, Jesus says; and as a matter of fact, I have gone ahead and done all the business that needs doing. But as long as you keep yourself out there in the dark, my doing of it might just as well never have happened: I have put a billion-dollar deal in your left hip pocket and you won't even move your hand to check it out.

Verse 20: "For every one who does evil (*phaúla*, bad things, vile things) hates the light and does not come to the light lest his deeds be exposed." Out in the darkness of our unbelief, we fear God and we hate God. Because we will look only at our own ugliness and not at Jesus' gracious, transforming beauty, we keep ourselves from the one thing that can save us—that has in fact saved us, even though we will not trust it. But . . . .

Verse 21. ". . . but he who does [___ _____] comes to the light that it may be clearly seen that his deeds have been done in God." As you can see, I have left out two words on purpose. What do you suppose they were? What is it that we all, sitting in the darkness with our *phaúla*, our vile deeds, our evil,

26

our ugliness, naturally assume Jesus to have said? Do not you, do not we all, bizarrely expect him to return, at the end of this rhapsody of gracious nonjudgment, to the old bait-and-switch offer of which we always suspected him? Are we not, in our guilt, fully prepared to hear him take back grace and reinstate law by saying, "but he who does *the good* comes to the light . . ."? But what does Jesus actually say? He says, "He who does *the truth (tēn alētheian)* comes to the light. . . ."

Do you see what that means? It means that we can come to the light no matter what our deeds have been. We are not required to clean up our act beforehand, and we are certainly not required to submit proof that the act will stay clean henceforth and forever. We are only required to *do the truth,* to bring our ugliness out of the dark into the light and to let the absolving acceptance of Jesus shine upon it. And we are to do that precisely in order that it may be clearly seen—by us, please note, because it was we, not God, who were in the dark—that *all* our deeds, good *and* bad, were done in God. Even our sins were committed in the Light who lightens everyone. Even in the moment of their commission, they were absolved by that Light. And except for our fearful, groundless hatred of the Light, we could have seen that all along.

To which fact, every Christian worship service bears witness. Sunday after Sunday we come into church with the same list of tiresome sins: our lust, our laziness, our anger, our jealousy, our pride. And Sunday after Sunday we begin our worship by confessing them. Why? What is the real purpose of Christian confession? Is it to present them to a God who doesn't know about them, or to haggle over them with a God who might possibly be talked into forgiving them? No. It is only to bring them to the light of Jesus and to see clearly that they were forgiven all along. It is only (to put it in the startling terms of the *Exultet,* the old Latin proclamation sung on Easter Eve) to force ourselves to rejoice over our sin because it has become the occasion of his grace—to see it as a *felix culpa,* a happy fault—and to wash away the whole sorry history of the world's transgressions in the absolving blood of the

Lamb. *"O certe necessarium Adae peccatum,"* the *Exultet* sings, "O certainly necessary sin of Adam," *"quae talem et tantum meruit habere redemptorem"*: "which deserved to have such and so great a Redeemer." We have always been home free, lightened even in the house of our sins by the Light of Light in whom they were all wrought. The only thing we do in confession is drag ourselves back in out of the dark that never was.

Let me end this chapter by delivering the third item I invoiced at the beginning, namely, verse 20 of chapter 3 of the Book of Revelation: "Behold, I stand at the door and knock. If any one hears my voice and opens the door, I will come in to him; and I will have supper *(deipnēsō)* with him, and he with me."

I choose this passage not because I intend to make a full commentary on the letters that Jesus, in a vision, told John the Divine to write to the seven churches in Asia but because it enables me to ring some changes on the image I just introduced of the house set in illusory darkness. In those early sections of Revelation, Jesus speaks to John in a vision of light: he is holding seven stars in his right hand and he is walking in the midst of seven golden lampstands. So much for the outer darkness: even as he stands out there on the world's front step and knocks—even there, outside the door of the swept and ordered house (Luke 11:25) he has provided for us in his death and resurrection, there is light; even those of us who perversely choose to love the darkness are standing in the Light. And so much for the threat of the seven devils worse than our first uncleanness (Luke 11:26) whom we might possibly invite in to make that house dark again: the judge of the world is on the doorstep and there isn't room for a single one of them.

For the judge who stands there is not alone. There is a crowd with him, and it isn't the cops. It is a party. It is all the guests at the Supper *(deipnon)* of the Lamb—plus the chefs and the caterer's crew and the musicians and the stars of the evening—all making an eternal racket, all pleading to bring the party into the house. And they have found our address not because they looked it up in the "books that were opened" at the last judgment before the great white throne (Rev. 20:12) —not because they examined our records and found us socially acceptable—but only because he showed them our names in the "other book that was opened" (Rev. 20:12, again): the Lamb's book of life.

Do you see? If he had looked us up in those *books,* we would all have been judged *according to our works* (Rev. 20:12, still), and the eternal party would never even have come down our street. But because he only looked us up in *the book*—because he came to save and not to judge, because in the Lamb's book we are all okay, all clothed with his righteousness, all drawn infallibly to himself by his being lifted up in death and resurrection—because of that and only because of that, he finds the door of every last one of us and lands the party on our porch. All we have to do is say yes to him and open the door. We do not have to earn the party; we already have the party. We do not have to understand the party, or conjure up good feelings about the party; we have only to enjoy the party. Everything else: the earning, the deserving, the knowing, the feeling—our records, our sins, even our sacred guilt— is irrelevant. "No man," Luther said, "can know or feel he is saved; he can only believe it." And he can only believe it because there is nothing left for him to do *but* believe it. It is already *here*. There is therefore *now* no condemnation. The Light *has come* into the world.

Even at the judgment, therefore, the gracious Light—the *Phōs hilarón*—is still the only game in town. When the Lamb stands at the door and knocks, only an inveterate nonsport would say, "Darkness, anyone?"

CHAPTER THREE

Death as the Engine of Judgment

*The Man Born Blind; the Good Shepherd; Jesus on Divorce
and Celibacy; Jesus and the Little Children;
the Rich Young Man*

For me, the parables of judgment begin at Matt. 19:1 (Aland no. 251)—the point at which the Matthean account of Jesus' final ministry in Judea supersedes the Lukan account of his last journey from Galilee to Jerusalem (Luke 9:51–18:34; Aland nos. 174-237). Nevertheless, the intervening passages (John 7:1–10:21) that Aland includes at nos. 238-250 deserve at least a few words, especially in view of my comments in the preceding chapter on the Johannine view of judgment.

This lengthy section of the Gospel of John deals with a visit Jesus made to Jerusalem for the feast of Tabernacles, and it buttresses nicely what I have been trying to establish as the gist of his teaching about judgment. In briefest outline, it goes as follows. At John 7:1, Jesus is in Galilee (as he is in Matt. 19:1 and Luke 9:51). His unbelieving brothers urge him to leave there and go to Judea in order to make a public demonstration of his ministry at the feast; but Jesus refuses, saying his time has not yet come. After his brothers depart without him, though, Jesus goes up to Jerusalem secretly and remains in hiding until the feast is about half over, at which point he begins to teach openly in the temple. He charges the Judean authorities (John 7:14-39) with not keeping the law and with trying to kill him; they, in turn, accuse him of having a demon. Since he knows they do not seriously think he is crazy but rather are furious over his heterodox assertions of authority— particularly over his healing of a sick man on the sabbath (John 5:9)—he flaunts that healing and tells them not to judge *(mē krínete)* by appearances but to judge right judgment *(dikaían krísin)*. The crowds listen eagerly to all this, but the chief priests and the Pharisees send officers to arrest him. Still, nothing happens at this point: the officers, just as impressed and/or confused by Jesus as the crowds are, return to their superiors without him. The authorities then debate the issue among themselves (John 7:40-52; fascinatingly, it is Nicodemus, the Pharisee whose visit to Jesus evoked the discourse in John 3:16ff., who stands up and defends him), and the arrest scheme goes temporarily into abeyance.

Jesus then speaks again (John 8:12), calling himself the light of the world and saying, "He who follows me will not walk in darkness but will have the light of life." (I make no comment here: the congruence of this entire passage with what I have so far set forth in this book should be obvious.) He accuses the authorities once again of judging *(krínete)* according to the flesh, but insists that he himself judges *(krínō)* no one. Yet even if he does judge *(krínō)*, he says, his judgment *(krísis)* is true *(alēthēs)* because it is nothing less than the judgment of the Father himself. The Judean authorities continue to bait him, but they still do not arrest him because, as John says, "his hour had not yet come" (8:20). Jesus then says plainly (8:26-28) that he has much to say about them and much to judge *(krínein)*, but that they will understand it all only when they have "lifted up the Son of man"—that is, only at his ultimate, gracious act of judgment, namely, the crucifixion. At these words, oddly, many believe *(epísteusan)* in him (8:30-36), and Jesus assures them that if they continue in his word, they will know the truth *(alētheian)* conveyed in his being lifted up, and that that truth will make them free.

Still, Jesus' argument with the authorities continues (John 8:37-47). He says they are seeking to kill him, but that if they were the children of Abraham, they would not act in such an un-Abrahamic way; they object that they are so Abraham's children—and God's too, for that matter. He says they are of their father the devil (8:48-59); they say again that he is the one who has a demon. He replies that he is not possessed— that he does not seek his own glory—but that there is One who does seek it, and it is that One who will be the ultimate judge *(ho krínōn)*. But then Jesus solemnly declares, "If any one keeps my word, he will never see death" (8:51). They say that proves he has a demon: even Abraham and the prophets died; who does he think he is? Jesus says they simply have not known God and he adds that Abraham himself, as a matter of fact, "rejoiced to see my day." They say he is too young to have known Abraham; he says, "before Abraham was, I am." They try to stone him for blasphemy; he, mysteriously, hides himself and goes out of the temple (8:52-59).

The next passage after these exchanges about judgment, light, and death is the vivid Johannine account of Jesus' acted parable of the Healing of the Man Born Blind (John 9:1-41; Aland no. 248). Once more, Jesus recurs to the theme that he is the light of the world; and once again — practically the minute after he restores the man's sight—the objections of the Pharisees resume in full force. They positively grill both the man and his parents, trying to prove the healing a fraud. In the end, though, when Jesus delivers his peroration to the healing (9:39), he does so by tying together, yet one more time, the themes of judgment and light: "For judgment *(kríma)* I came into the world," he says, "that those who do not see may see, and that those who see may become blind."

Then, in John 10:1-18, he goes on to tie the knot between judgment and death: he speaks of himself as the good shepherd who lays down his life for the sheep. He proclaims, in other words, that his death is the operative device by which the reconciling judgment of God works—that the crucifixion is God's last word on the subject of sin, the final sentence that will make the world one flock under one gracious shepherd. Nevertheless, as John notes in the concluding paragraph (10:19-21) of this entire section, the net result of everything Jesus has said and done at the feast of Tabernacles is a continuing division among the Judean authorities. Some still say he is possessed; others are disposed to take him seriously. But those who favor getting rid of Jesus are about to prevail. The long narration has admirably advanced the plot: after only a few more confrontations—and in particular after the raising of Lazarus from the dead (11:1-53)—the authorities will be ready to arrest him as a threat to public safety. Because they love darkness more than light, they see Jesus' preaching of judgment only through the dark glasses of their fear that he will provoke the Romans to take action and destroy both the temple and the nation. As Caiaphas the high priest later says in unwitting prophecy (11:50), they decide that "it is better that one man die for the people than that the whole nation perish." And so John himself ties the ultimate knot in this paradoxical tapestry of judgment: even though they will not accept the light that Jesus brings them, their very effort to extinguish that light on the cross will become an instrument of grace. Even they themselves, therefore, will have in some sense "done the truth": their worst will have been done in the Light that brings everything to its best.

With that much (or that little) said about the Johannine intermezzo, it is time to return to Matt. 19:1. Jesus, as I noted, is in Galilee; but he departs immediately for the region of Judea beyond the Jordan and large crowds follow him. This passage corresponds, of course, with Luke 9:51, where Jesus leaves Galilee to begin his last journey to Jerusalem. But in Luke, it takes many chapters—nine, in fact, all devoted to the parables of grace I have expounded in the previous volume*—to reach the point (Luke 18:18) that Matthew arrives at only verses later at Matt. 19:16. At first, therefore, it might seem that there is a large discrepancy here between the Lukan and the Matthean chronologies. Nevertheless, it is possible to argue that Luke's nine chapters do not represent as long a time period as

*The Parables of Grace (Grand Rapids: Eerdmans, 1988).

they seem to. Since only *two* sabbaths (Luke 13:14 and 14:1) are recorded in the whole section, it just might be that the entire passage represents a space of three weeks or less. If that is so, it fits in nicely with my choice of colors for the parables of grace and the parables of judgment. Because in both Matthew and Luke, we are now very nearly up to Palm Sunday (it occurs in Luke 19 and Matt. 21): we are, in short, only days away from Jesus' death and resurrection. Accordingly, just as Jesus' certainty of an early crucifixion colored the parables of grace with the purple of passion and death, so that same sense of the imminence of the cross produces the white heat of the parables of judgment.

As a matter of fact, there is even an image in Scripture that corroborates this dominance of death over the parables. In the Lukan account of the transfiguration (Luke 9:28-36), Moses and Elijah appear in glory and speak with Jesus about his *éxodos* (that is, his death and resurrection) which he was about to accomplish *(hēn émellen plēroún)* in Jerusalem. Do you see? It is as if Jesus has gone up on the mountain to consult not one but two doctors—two specialists in the dispensation of the mystery—who tell him he has less than a month to live. From that point on, therefore, his mind has only one thing uppermost in it: death and resurrection. To my way of thinking, that has two tremendous consequences for the study of the parables. Not only does death-resurrection become the most likely *leitmotiv*—the sovereign recurring theme—in his composition of both the parables of grace and the parables of judgment; it also becomes (or should become) the principal interpretative device for their exposition.

I note those consequences here for a reason. At this point in the Gospel narrative, all three synoptic writers are doing two things. Principally, of course, they are preparing to head into the passion/resurrection narrative which, as I have said, is the *terminus ad quem* of all four Gospels. But incidentally, they are also trying to work in the remaining bits and pieces about Jesus they have not so far included. They have on hand, as it were, a slim packet of index cards with unused words and actions of

Jesus noted on them, and they are concerned to put check marks on as many of them as possible. Accordingly, as I come in the course of my exposition to what seems to be extraneous, or at least arbitrarily inserted material (which I shall do very shortly indeed, in Matt. 19:3-12), I shall make every effort to give it a death-resurrection interpretation. And I shall do that on two grounds. The first is that Jesus (with the cross uppermost in his mind) may well have said or done the very things the Gospel writers attribute to him at those very points in his ministry. The second is that even if he did not, the writers themselves may well have inserted them where they did for the same reason: they may have seen, in these apparently moralistic or otherwise out-of-synch passages, a death-resurrection coloring that warranted their inclusion.

In any event, Matt. 19:3-12 becomes the first instance of a seemingly irrelevant passage that turns out, on examination, to be more germane than it looks. Some Pharisees come to Jesus and ask him (*peirázontes autón:* tempting him, putting him to the test) a leading and tricky question. "Is it lawful," they inquire, "for a man to put away his wife for any and every reason?" It is not clear from the text just why they put the question this way. Perhaps the most likely interpretation is that they suspected Jesus of being a "liberal" about the law (he did, after all, break the sabbath) and hoped he would say something incriminatingly loose on the subject of matrimony.

Whatever their reason, Jesus comes back at them with a reply that is devastatingly strict. Quoting Genesis, he attacks *them* for the very tampering with the law of which they hoped to convict him. By the decree of the Torah, he tells them, a man and his wife are one; what therefore God has joined together, let no one put asunder. Jesus knows (see Matt. 5:31) that they have long taken the view that giving a wife a "letter of putting away" (an *apostásion*) was permissible—that the inconvenience of the law could be mitigated in cases where the inconvenience of the wife became excessive. And sure enough, they take the bait. They quote the Torah back at him from Deut. 24:1: "Why then," they ask, "did Moses command us to give a wife who is put away a letter of *apostasíou?*" But Jesus, shrewd rabbinical controversalist that he is, is ready for them. "I quoted from Genesis," he tells them, "and since Genesis comes first in the Torah, that means that my quote shows God's intention from the beginning. What you gave me from Deuteronomy comes later: it's nothing more than an accommodation to your resistance to the truth (*tēn sklērokardían hymõn,* your hardness of heart)."

Jesus then adds a verse that has always been one of the most difficult and problematical in Scripture: "And I say to you that whoever puts away his wife, *except for harlotry (mē epí porneía),* and marries another, commits adultery" (Matt. 19:9). I have nothing to say about this so-called Matthean exception, other than to note that it is indeed an exception. For one thing, it is at odds with the rest of what Jesus is saying at this point (the parallel passages in Mark 10:11-12 and Luke 18:18 offer no such exception to the uncompromising strictness of his reply to the Pharisees); for another, the church's occasional, and foolish, enactment of it into canon law has served almost no purpose beyond providing an excuse for cashiering marriages that a little Christian forgiveness might have saved. Because whatever it means and wherever it came from, the phrase itself is exceptionally ill-suited to its context. Throughout this passage, Jesus is intentionally taking a hard line; therefore it is precisely the hardness of his reply, not this inconsistent exception to it, that must occupy the interpreter's attention.

What then is my interpretation? Simply this. Jesus is zeroing in on the Pharisees' desire to establish their own righteousness—to be winners, successful livers of lawful lives—by whittling the law down to the size of their own less-than-successful obedience. But that, he tells them in effect, just won't wash. The law still stands in all its righteous, unflinching obligation. And he goes on to imply what Paul was to say later and more fully in Romans, namely, that if they take their stand on the law they will simply be condemned by the law because no one can ever really keep it. But not to worry, he tells them in effect; because if you take your stand on my saving cross—if you will only believe me when I say I came not to judge but to save, not to examine records but to erase them, not to enforce the charges contained in the law of commandments and ordinances but to nail them all to my cross (Eph. 2:15; Col. 2:14)—then you will be out of the court system forever. For you will have taken your stand on the truth about yourself—on the truth that all your deeds, whatever they were, were done in the light of my absolving death and resurrection —and that truth, by your simple trust in my word that it is already true, will make you free.

Do you see what that means? It means that we are saved not by our successes but in and through our failures—not by our lives but in our deaths. For our so-called lives and our vaunted successes cannot be saved. They are nothing but suits of obsolete armor, ineffective moral and spiritual contraptions we have climbed into to avoid facing the one thing that *can* save us: our vulnerability. Jesus is not the least bit interested in saving the President of the United States or the Archbishop of Canterbury or the Duchess of Kent; he is not even interested in saving the Father of Six Children, or the Mother on Welfare. He does not care beans about the titles and roles we assign to ourselves in our successes, any more than he cares beans about the names we call ourselves in our failures. It is *us* he saves, not our lives. It is the *person* he dies for, not the suit of clothes in which the person hides from the bare truth about himself. He does not save you or me as we dress ourselves up at high noon on a good day; he saves us only as we stumble naked and uncombed from lumpy mattress to cold shower after a long, hard night—as, that is, we limp in faith from the bed of our death, through the blood of the cross, to the joy of his resurrection.

If you find that a bit much to wring out of Jesus' *obiter dicta* on the subject of matrimony, you have plenty of company. It isn't only you and the Pharisees who found less in his remarks than I claim to have discovered. Jesus' own best friends are with you all the way. In Matt. 19:10-12—after the

Pharisees have presumably walked off in disgust—the disciples proceed to miss his point by a country mile. "Gee whiz, Lord," they say to him in effect, "if that's how tough your marriage standards are, shouldn't we just advise people not to get married at all?" Their literal minds, you see, have gone to the only destination they can think of: celibacy. But Jesus refuses to let them stay there. He does the old, master-teacher's trick of dividing himself in two and quietly crouching down behind them before shoving them over from the front—and then he sends them sprawling. "Dummies!" he says to them. "Haven't you heard what I've been saying? Not getting married is no solution either. That's just more fiddling with the law—more of the same, silly business of trying to win the game by shaving the rules. Don't you see that I'm not going to save winners at all? Besides, who would volunteer for the job of being eunuchs like that just to make a moral buck? Only one more little club of losers who thought they had figured out a way of winning—only a bunch of select types who were either born without *cojones* or cut them off because they thought that society, or maybe even God, had decided it was a neat idea. Well, if you like that sort of thing, more power to you; me, I've had it with all these private success clubs and their nifty admissions requirements. What I'm into now is a *catholic* salvation: one that's going to work on *failure only*—one that's going to include the whole world because the only thing it's going to need will be the one thing that everybody has, namely, death. Not life. Not success. And certainly not the ability to draw to some moral inside straight. Just the *cojones* to admit the truth that they're dead, and to trust me to take care of everything else."

That, I gather, you finally find a bit more than too much. I apologize. But not for myself alone. I had help: Jesus, after all, was the one who brought up the subject of castration to begin with. Relax, though: time now for a return to seemliness on both our parts: Jesus' Blessing of Little Children (Matt. 19:13-15).

The brief account of this often-portrayed episode is found

in all three synoptic Gospels. Moreover, it is present in all three in the same context: it occurs not long before Palm Sunday and Good Friday. Therefore, in line with my principle that what was uppermost in Jesus' mind should be uppermost in ours as we interpret him, I ask you to set aside all the sentimental Victorian depictions of this episode that you may have in your head and think about it solely in terms of Jesus' death as the gracious judgment rendered by the Light of the world.

For Victorian sentimentality is precisely what all those intellectually loosey-goosey pictures of Jesus blessing a mixed bag of tiny tykes are actually about. The modern world's wishful view of childhood as a blessed, innocent state—and thus of children as fundamentally unfallen creatures — is a late nineteenth-century invention. Prior to that time, children were not only seen (wisely) as no less sinful than anyone else; they were also seen (sadly) as imperfect, sawed-off adults who needed little more than to have their imperfections beaten out of them and their education beaten into them. Children were seen as losers, in other words—and childhood was considered a state that no sane child (or adult) would choose to stay in for one minute more than was necessary.

I bring that up again (I made the same point in my previous book, *The Parables of Grace*) because it is crucial here. Jesus is not simply being the gentle Scoutmaster in this passage; he sees an opportunity to make a death-forgiveness-judgment-light buck and he takes it. Watch.

"Children *(paidía)* were brought to Jesus," Matthew says (19:13), "that he might lay his hands on them and pray." So far, so good. But then the disciples—sharing the perennial, pre-Victorian view that children are little losers with whom the Important Rabbi should not be bothered—rebuke the people who brought them. "C'mon," they seem to be saying to the importunate parents, "get these kids out of here; the Master has bigger fish to fry." But Jesus, in effect, rebukes *them* (19:14) for being the same thickheaded point-missers they had just been on the subject of eunuchs. Little losers, he tells them—the last, the least, and the dead (of which children are the perfect paradigm)—are what his plan of salvation is all about. "Let *(áphete)* the children come to me and do not hinder them," he says, "for to such belongs the kingdom of heaven." But what he is thinking is, How many times do I have to say this? How long is it going to take you to catch on to the fact that I don't work with winners? I am not in the business of saving people's questionably successful lives. I am in the business of being a loser myself and of offering them, in my crucifixion, a chance to turn the absolutely certain unsuccess of their death into pure gold. So what am I going to do now? I am going to *show* them, that's what. Right now. With these very children. And so, as Matthew notes, "he laid his hands on them and went away."

Notice the details of the account. The word he uses to rebuke the disciples, "Let *(áphete)* the children come . . . ," is one of the most weighty in the New Testament. The verb *aphiénai* (root, *aph-*; noun, *áphesis*) is not only the ordinary word for *let, permit, allow, suffer, dismiss;* it is also, in the other half of its many uses, the ordinary word for *forgive*. It is the word Jesus uses when he has the farmer in the parable of the Wheat and the Weeds tell the servants to "let *(áphete)* both grow together until the harvest"; it is the word he utters from the cross when he says, "Father, forgive *(áphes)* them"; and it is the word he tells us to use when we pray his prayer: "Forgive *(áphes)* us our trespasses as we forgive *(aphékamen)* those who trespass against us." The word, in short, carries within itself a profound pun by which forgiveness and permission constantly dog each other's steps. Even if Jesus did not intend the pun, therefore, it still lurks in the passage at hand by the inspiration of the Spirit—and it tempts the interpreter mightily.

But that is not all. The rebuke is also a judgment. "Let the children *(paidía)* come" is a condemnation of all those—disciples, Pharisees, you, me—who love the darkness of our success more than the light of failure that streams from the Holy Child *(pais:* Acts 4:27). The judgment, you see, is precisely what Jesus said it was in John 3:19: that the light of death and resurrection has come into the world but that hardly anyone wants it because we are all busy rubbing the wet sticks of our lives together in the dark. Grace doesn't sell; you can hardly even give it away, because it works only for losers and no one wants to stand in their line. The world of winners will buy case lots of moral advice, grosses of guilt-edged prohibitions, skids of self-improvement techniques, and whole truckloads of transcendental hot air. But it will not buy free forgiveness because *that* threatens to let the riffraff into the Supper of the Lamb. And therefore the world of winners is judged already (*édē kékritai,* John 3:18) because it will not believe in the name of the only begotten Child (*pais,* again: Acts 4:27) whom God raised from the dead—in the Loser of God who, in the fullness of his permitting, forgiving love, goes ahead and lays his hands on a bunch of grubby little kids and says, "There! That's what I have in mind."

So the Blessing of the Children becomes an acted parable second to none: a parable of grace and forgiveness and light—and a parable, above all, of the inescapable judgment that Mercy pronounces on a world that won't even put mercy on the bottom of its list. In addition, though, it becomes the totally apposite, utterly logical preface to the next passage in Matthew, namely, the acted parable of the Rich Young Man.

This episode (Matt. 19:16-22) likewise appears in all three synoptics. Matthew and Mark identify the man who eagerly comes to Jesus as young and rich—a yuppie if there ever was one. Luke introduces him simply as "a ruler" (*árchōn*) and leaves the reader in the dark as to his age. In any case, they all agree on the question that this go-getter has in mind (I conflate the accounts): "Good Teacher," he asks, "what good deed must I do to inherit eternal life?" The man, you see, is already a success as far as this world is concerned. But now . . . well, let us supply him with some adapted lines from Auden's *Caliban to the Audience* to flesh out his innermost thoughts.

He feels a call to higher, finer things. "Oh, yes," he sighs, "I have had what once I would have called success. I moved the vices out of the city into a chain of reconditioned lighthouses. I introduced statistical methods into the Liberal Arts.

I revived the country dances and installed electric stoves in the mountain cottages. I saved democracy by buying steel. . . . But the world is no better and it is now quite clear to me that there is nothing to be done with such a ship of fools adrift on a sugarloaf sea in which it is going very soon and suitably to founder. Deliver me, dear Teacher, from the tantrums of my telephones and the whispers of my secretaries . . . deliver me from these helpless agglomerations of dishevelled creatures with their bed-wetting, vomiting, weeping bodies, their giggling, fugitive, disappointing hearts, and their scrawling, blotted, misspelled minds, to whom I have so foolishly tried to bring the light they do not want . . . translate me, bright Angel, from this hell of inert and ailing matter, growing steadily senile in a time forever immature, to that blessed realm, so far above the twelve impertinent winds and the four unreliable seasons, that Heaven of the Really General Case where, tortured no longer by three dimensions and immune to temporal vertigo, Life turns into Light, absorbed for good into the permanently stationary, completely self-sufficient, absolutely reasonable One."

Now do you see the man's problem as Jesus saw it? This fellow is a winner who will not give up trying to win. To be sure, he has gotten beyond mere worldly winning to a desire for Something Better; but he cannot for the life of him imagine the pursuit of that Spiritual Something by any other means than still more winning. He is sure there must be techniques for making a spiritual profit just as there were for making a temporal one, and he has come to Jesus to study them.

Jesus, however, has his number. "What's with all this talk about good?" he asks him (Matt. 19:17). "Nobody's good, and nobody's going to be. Maybe I'm good; but my goodness looks so much like badness that people can't even stand the thought of it. And God, of course, really is good, but not in any way you can hope to imitate. So just knock off this goodness routine and listen to what I'm trying to tell you."

Time to shift for a moment here to Mark 10:19 and Luke 18:20. Matthew's version of what Jesus says next has an element of unparadoxical moralism in it—an element that the other two Gospels (with greater logic, I think) leave out. For what I think Jesus sets out to do after saying that goodness eludes us all is to challenge the young man. He wants him to take an honest look at just how successful he has actually been at practicing the goodness he thinks is the answer to his problems. In other words (if you will pardon the anachronism), Jesus is hoping for a little Pauline insight from him—hoping he will see that the law can save no one because the law can be kept by no one. So he says to him, "Hey! You know the commandments: 'Don't kill; Don't commit adultery; Don't steal; Don't bear false witness; Don't defraud; Honor your father and mother.' Why don't you take a really good look at them?" Jesus, you see, is handing the rich young man a straight-line. And the yuppie is supposed to respond with something like, "Oh, I get you: I haven't really been a winner even at those things, so why should I run around looking for even more good things I can be a failure at?"

Alas, though, the gambit doesn't work. This young man cannot even conceive of losing, so he simply cuts Jesus off with, "Oh, Teacher, I've done all those things perfectly ever since I was a kid. Why don't you give me a really hard, grown-up assignment?" But then, as Mark says (10:21), "Jesus looked at him, and loved him." You poor, amiable sap, he thinks to himself. I like you a lot, Harry. More than you'll ever know. But it just doesn't work that way. You try to save your life like that, you'll only lose it. You have to lose, l-o-s-e, lose your life to save it. Still, I'll give you a shot at what I mean, just to prove I love you.

And so, with consummate understatement, Jesus gently breaks the Good News to him. "You only have to do one simple little thing, Harry: sell everything you have and give it to the poor. That will take care of getting your treasury of merits off your back. Then come and follow me into my death." And at that saying, Mark says, the young man got very gloomy in the face and went off in a deep depression because "he had great possessions" — because, that is, he just couldn't bear the thought of being a loser.

The saddest part of the whole thing, though, is that he turned his back on the only really good piece of news he would ever hear, because in something under threescore years and ten, all that great stuff of his — all those *ktḗmata pollá,* those many goods, worldly or spiritual, physical or intellectual—would be taken from him anyway. And so would all his terrible stuff as well: the whole pile of his unacknowledged failures, the ratty tissue of his irretrievable relationships and second-rate loves. *All* of his achievements—his successful virtues as well as his success-loving vices — would someday go whistling into the ultimate no-win situation, the final, redeeming unsuccess of death. And the next saddest part of it is that in spite of this acted parable of the Rich Young Man—in spite of Jesus' clear insistence that no winner will ever do anything but lose—you and I go right on blithely trying to win. If it is not financial success that keeps us from the saving emptiness of Jesus on the cross, it is moral success, intellectual success, emotional success, or spiritual success. We simply will not lose; and without losing, we will never, ever, win.

Which is why, in terms of both Matthew's Gospel and this book, it is time to start a fresh chapter. Matthew is headed for the great parable of losers who win, the Laborers in the Vineyard (Matt. 20:1-16; Aland no. 256); and I want to use his next section (19:23-30; Aland no. 255: On Riches and the Rewards of Discipleship) as a bridge to it.

So as they say in books designed for the little children to whom the kingdom of heaven belongs, turn the page.

CHAPTER FOUR

A Rhapsody of Unsuccess

*The Curse of Riches; the Eye of the Needle;
the Laborers in the Vineyard*

After the rich young man leaves the scene, Jesus makes a remark that needs more careful exposition than it often gets. The Gospel accounts (Matt. 19:23; Mark 10:23; Luke 18:24) differ in some significant details, so I take the liberty of giving you all three. In Matthew, he says to his disciples, "Amen, I say to you, it will be hard *(dyskólōs)* for a rich man *(ploúsios)* to enter the kingdom of heaven." In Mark, he "looks around" and he says to the disciples, "How hard it will be for those who have riches *(hoi ta chrēmata* — goods — *échontes)* to enter the kingdom of God." But in Luke, Jesus "looks at *him*" (that is, at the young man going sadly into the sunset of his successful life) and he says, to no one in particular, "How hard it is for those who have riches [the words are identical with Mark's version] to enter the kingdom of God."

On the whole, I am disposed to soft-pedal the Matthean account at this point. I find Mark more convincing as far as the words of Jesus are concerned, and I think Luke is more nearly right about the stage business with which Jesus delivers them. In all three Gospels, of course, this saying has judgmental aspects not only on its face but also in its general context, namely, as part of the buildup to Holy Week and to the specific parables of judgment that Jesus will deliver before his death.

45

But in Matthew, it seems not only judgmental but unfairly so: "Amen, I say to you, *it will be hard.* . . ." When the saying is put that way, it sounds as if Jesus is little more than a new Moses issuing a new and harsher law to the effect that the mere possession of wealth is offensive enough to warrant exclusion from the kingdom. His words, in short, seem a bit too ser-mon-on-the-mountish for this late in his ministry. (Not that I think that either these words or the Sermon on the Mount must necessarily be taken simply as legislation imposing a new morality; even in Matthew, both are more paradoxical than that. It's just that the prescriptive tone he gives them ractically shoves the interpreter into a legalistic corner.)

In the other two synoptics, though, Jesus' words sound more like lament than law. "How hard it is . . ." is not an edict that says, "I will make it tough on the rich"; it is a sad, loving commentary on how tough the rich make it for themselves. It is indeed a judgment; but it is a judgment that is precisely par-allel to his lament over the city in Matt. 23:37-39 and Luke 13:34-35: "O Jerusalem, Jerusalem, killing the prophets and stoning those who are sent to you! How often would I have gathered your children together as a hen gathers her brood under her wings, and you would not! Behold, your house is forsaken!" It is a judgment, in other words, utterly in line with the prin-ciple of inclusion before exclusion that I set down at the outset as the key to the parables of judgment: it is gracious, loving ac-ceptance mourning the rejection of acceptance. Jesus has already included both the city and the rich young man within the grace of his saving death: except for their own self-estrangement, both are loved and both are uncondemned. It is only their rejection of his acceptance—which, please note, is the sole Gospel basis for condemnation—that puts them in darkness rather than light.

But that is not the only reason I prefer Mark's and Luke's recounting of words and stage business at this point; I also think that their versions make the best sense of the next remark that all three Gospel writers assign to Jesus, namely, "It is eas-ier for a camel to go through the eye of a needle than for a rich man to enter the kingdom of God."

It is common expository practice to suggest that in these words Jesus is referring to some actual narrow gate or passageway in the city of Jerusalem. If that is so, the meaning is plain enough: a fully loaded camel, with bundles of goods strapped to its sides, cannot get through the Eye of the Needle Gate without being unloaded; likewise, a rich young man has to get rid of his baggage before . . . etc. Still, the passage makes just as good sense if it is taken as plain old Oriental hyperbole: just as you can't stuff a camel through an opening designed to take only a thread, so you can't get someone who has a great, fat, successful life to volunteer to go through the narrow eye of lastness and death. Both interpretative gambits, therefore, come to the same point: Jesus' plan of salvation works only with the last, the lost, the least, the little, and the dead; the living, the great, the successful, the found, and the first simply will not consent to the radical slimming down that Jesus, the Needle of God, calls for if he is to pull them through into the kingdom.

Actually, therefore, this strict-sounding pronouncement of Jesus turns out to be more descriptive than prescriptive—as do a good many others. In Matt. 7:13-14, for example, he says, "Enter in by the narrow gate; for wide is the gate and easy is the road that leads to destruction *(apóleian)*, and many there are who travel it. But narrow is the gate and difficult the road that leads to life, and few there are who find it." These words, like the words "how hard it is . . . ," have often been read as a new, wrenching turn of the law's screw intended to keep nearly everybody out of the kingdom. But on a wider and fairer reading, neither they nor the remark about the camel and the eye of the needle should be given such an interpretation. Both should be read under the grand rubric of John 12:22: "I, if I be lifted up from the earth, will draw *all* to me." Jesus the Needle is willing to sew up the salvation of every last son of Adam and every last daughter of Eve by threading them into the eye of his death—into the spear-wound in his side, if you will—just as Jesus the Divine Vacuum Cleaner will suck everyone who isn't obsessed with the wide gate of success right smack into the kingdom through the narrow slot of his failure on the cross. Accordingly, all we have to do is *let go*—let go of everything that is not the slim thread of our lastness and lostness, and let go of every effort to walk the easy road of winning—and upon that letting go, he will draw us home.

Thus, while the sentence he pronounces on those who will not let go is indeed a judgment, it describes and mourns their condition more than it prescribes and gloats over their fate. It is sadder than it is stern, more loving than it is condemning. "Oh, damn!" Jesus says, stamping a lover's furious foot: "Why won't you come? Why won't you let me draw you? Why do you insist on loving the darkness when you're already standing in the light? How can you not know the things that belong to your peace?" (Luke 19:42). And therefore Hell (*apóleia,* destruction—the ultimate destination of overloaded camels and fatheaded finders of the wide road of success) is as real as it is unnecessary and as eternal (so it seems, God help us) as the Love that will not let go even of those who won't stop hanging on to the successes that are destroying them. It is a perpetual Mexican standoff between the Loser who has won it all and the Winners who cannot stand the thought of losing. It is, in short, *hell.*

The disciples, however, are no more ready to think about such things than the rest of us are. "They were exceedingly astonished," the Gospel says (Mark 10:26), and they said to him, "Then who can be saved?" But then, Mark adds, "Jesus looked at them."

Once again, the stage business is no less important than the lines. The *looks* that Jesus uses or implies in this scene are worth a thousand words. He looks at the young man walking dejectedly away; he looks at the disciples in their incomprehension; and all the while, in his mind's eye, he looks at his own impending death. Moreover, in every one of these looks, the attentive watcher of the play senses the sad wrath of his love. Perhaps for the first time, Jesus hints at his growing realization that what he is asking of the world is simply too much —that it really is an impossible invitation. "You're right," he says after he has held the look for the extra beat needed to convey an inward resignation; "with men, this is impossible" (Matt. 19:26). Grace, he realizes, is the last thing the world will buy.

But grace, he also realizes, is the only thing that will work on the world as it so sadly is. "An eye for an eye" won't work because all it does is double the number of eyeless people. Retribution won't take evil out of the world; it will simply perpetuate it in spades. A judgment that works only by punishing sinners and rewarding the righteous produces all hell and no kingdom: there are just too many sinners, and there are no righteous. The only thing that's going to get evil out of the world is for him to take it into himself on the cross—to drop it down the black hole of his death—and to make a new creation by the power of his resurrection. And so after thinking it all through, he adds, "but with God, all things are possible" —even the impossibility of grace.

Most of the disciples, apparently, remain stymied by all this; but Peter—dear old dim, bright Peter—suddenly gets at least a glimmer of what Jesus is talking about. Not a clear vision, mind you, for Peter goes nowhere with it at this point and he forgets it almost completely at the trial and crucifixion. But he does see for a moment that Jesus is talking about losing, not winning, as the touchstone of salvation. He says (Mark 10:28), "Look, we have left *(aphēkamen!)* everything and followed you." Matthew has him add, "what will that get us therefore?" but since Mark and Luke leave this out, I think we can give him credit for just a tad less denseness than Matthew suggests. However dimly he perceives it, Peter does sense that saving lives is not what Jesus is up to. He smells, if you will, the reek of death; and he notices, in a way he never noticed before, that it does not seem to bother Jesus—that, in fact, Jesus is convinced it smells like roses. And therefore when he says, "We have left everything . . . ," he is not just looking for a payback. Rather, he is saying—in the very thick of all the impossibilities his conscious mind perceives—something much more like, "Look, I can't say I understand you, but I'm with you all the way." He is anticipating, in other words—with just as much sincerity and just as little self-knowledge—what he will say later, shortly before his denial of Jesus: "Lord, I am ready to go with you to prison and to death" (Luke 22:33).

Jesus, grateful for his sincerity and going gently on his lack of insight, gives him a soft answer with a hard core. Not budging an inch from his insistence that grace works only by loss, he says to Peter and to all the disciples (I am following Mark 10:29-31 here), "Amen, I say to you, there is no one who has left *(aphēken)* house or brothers or sisters or mother or father or children or lands for my sake and for the Gospel, who will not receive a hundredfold now in this time, houses and brothers and sisters and mothers and children and lands, *with persecutions* [italics mine], and in the age to come, eternal life. But many that are first shall be last, and the last first."

I shall resist (almost) the temptation to read those italicized words back into the preceding list of goods to be restored "now in this time." I shall not spend more than this one sentence reminding you that twentieth-century psychology has taught us only too well that it is precisely our possession, gained or regained, of mothers and fathers, children and siblings and stuff, that lies at the root of most of our problems. I simply point out that, in Mark, the awfulness of saving grace—the dreadfulness of a Love that will not take us *out* of our troubles, but instead insists on saving us *in and through* them—is succinctly conveyed by the phrase "with persecutions." The other two Gospels, of course, introduce that awfulness just as definitely when they quote Jesus' words about the first and the last; but they do so out of the blue, as it were, without the preparation that Mark supplies. Why they left them out (both, after all, had access to Mark) is a puzzle. Matthew, perhaps, felt that the upcoming parable of the Laborers in the Vineyard more than made up for the omission; Luke's reasons are simply a mystery. In any case, it is to that very parable that Matthew turns next; so let me get straight to it, expounding it as the rhapsody of unsuccess that I, along with him, take it to be.

The Laborers in the Vineyard (Matt. 20:1-16)

(Classroom Teacher's Version)

Since you have all read the assignment . . . (much eye-rolling, some guilty looks) . . . I shall tell you the story anyway.

There was a man who owned a vineyard. His operation was not on the scale of E & J Gallo, but it was quite respectable: let us put him in the Robert Mondavi class. We first see this gentleman on the evening of the second Sunday in October. September has been a perfect month — hot and dry, bringing the grapes to 20° brix — but his meteorological service tells him that the weather is about to turn into cold soup. So what does our friend Robert do? He gets up first thing Monday morning, goes down to what passes for the local hiring hall and contracts for as much day labor as he can pick up. Unfortunately, every other grower in the neighborhood uses the same weather reports, so he has to promise higher pay to attract the workers he needs: $120 for the day is the figure that finally guarantees him a crew.

I see a hand up. Yes, Virginia?

No, Virginia, $120 is not a ridiculous figure. A *denarius* was a day's pay; I have simply taken the liberty of making it a good day's pay. A penny a day may have been alright for the translators of the KJV, but this is 1989.

Anyway, Robert loads his crew into a couple of old school buses and puts them to work, chop-chop. Just before nine A.M., though, he gets another weather bulletin. They have moved the start of the three weeks of rain from Wednesday back to Tuesday: he has one day, not two, to get the harvest in. Out he goes at nine, therefore—and with increasing panic at noon and at three—to hire on still more hands. Each time he succeeds in rounding up all the available help, giving them the by now practiced line that he is Robert Mondavi, the famous payer of top dollar who is also Mr. Fairness himself: whatever is right, they will get.

It's a huge harvest, though, and with only one hour left

before dark, Robert realizes he won't get it in on time without still more help. So out he goes again, but the hiring hall is closed by now and the village square has only its usual crowd of up-to-the-minute losers hanging out in a haze of smoke. You know the types: lots of leather, some girls (and their boyfriends) with more mousse than brains, six-packs everywhere, and music that ruptures eardrums. What the hell, Robert thinks in desperation: it's worth at least a try. So he walks up to the group, ostentatiously switches off the offending ghetto-blaster, and goes into his spiel: he's Robert Mondavi; he's famous and he's fair; they could probably use a buck; so what do they think? What they think, of course, is also What the hell: whatever he wants them to do, it won't take long; and whatever he pays, at least it's a couple more six-packs for the night. Off they go.

Now then: run your mind over the story so far. I'm sure you know exactly what happens each time one of those new batches of workers gets dropped off at the vineyard. Before they pick even a single grape, they make sure they find out from the workers already on the job the exact per diem amount on which Robert Mondavi is basing his chances at the Guinness Book of World Records. And since they are—like the rest of the human race—inveterate bookkeepers, they take the $120 figure, divide it by twelve and multiply it by the number of hours they'll be working. Then and only then do they lay hand to grape, secure in the knowledge that they will be getting, respectively, $100, $70, $40, and $10.

Robert, however, has a surprise for them. At the end of the day, he is a happy man. With his best and biggest harvest on its way to the stemmer-crusher, he feels expansive—and a little frisky. So he says to his foreman, "I have a wild idea. I'm going to fill the pay envelopes myself; but when you give them out, I want you to do it backwards, beginning with the last ones hired."

Once again, I'm sure, you know what happens. When the first girl with purple hair gets her envelope and walks away opening it, she finds six crisp, new twenties inside. What does she do?

No, Virginia, put your hand down. She does *not* go back and report the overage; she just keeps on walking—fast.

But when her shirt-open-to-the-waist boyfriends catch up with her and tell her they got $120, too . . . well, dear old human nature triumphs again: they cannot resist going back and telling everybody else what jerks they were for sweating a whole day in the hot sun when they could have made the same money for just an hour's work.

The entail of Adam's transgression being what it is, however, the workers who were on the job longer come up with yet another example of totally unoriginal sin. On hearing that Robert Mondavi is now famous for paying $120 *an hour,* they put their mental bookkeeping machinery into reverse and floor the pedal. And what do they then come up with? O frabjous joy! They conclude that they are now about to become the proud possessors of, in order, $480, or $840, or even—bless you, Robert Mondavi—$1,440.

But Robert, like God, is only crazy, not stupid. Like God, he has arranged for their recompense to be based only on the weird goodness he is most famous for, not on the just deserts they have infamously imagined for themselves: every last envelope, they find, has six (6) twenties in it; no more for those who worked all day, and no less for those who didn't.

Which, of course, goes down like Gatorad for the last bunch hired, like dishwater for the next-to-the-last, like vinegar for the almost-first, and like hot sulfuric acid for the first-of-all. Predictably, therefore — on the lamebrained principle that those who are most outraged should argue the case for those who are less so (wisdom would have whispered to them, "Reply in anger and you'll make the best speech you'll ever regret") — the sweatiest and the most exhausted decide to give Robert a hard time. "Hey, man," they say; "you call this a claim to fame? Those punks over there only worked one hour and we knocked ourselves out all day. How come you made them equal to us?"

Robert, however, has his speech in his pocket. "Look, Pal," he says. (Incidentally, the Greek word in the parable is *hetaíre,* which is a distinctly unfriendly word for "friend." In three of its four uses in the New Testament—here, and to the man without the wedding garment in the King's Son's Wedding, and to Judas at the betrayal—it comes off sounding approximately like "Buster.") "Look, Pal," he tells the spokesman for all the bookkeepers who have gagged on this parable for two thousand years, "Don't give me *agita*. You agreed to $120 a day, I gave you $120 a day. Take it and get out of here before I call the cops. If I want to give some pot-head in Gucci loafers the same pay as you, so what? You're telling me I can't do what I want with my own money? I'm supposed to be a stinker because you got your nose out of joint? All I did was have a fun idea. I decided to put the last first and the first last to show you there are no insiders or outsiders here: when I'm happy, everybody's happy, no matter what they did or didn't do. I'm not asking you to like me, Buster; I'm telling you to enjoy me. If you want to mope, that's your business. But since the only thing it'll get you is a lousy disposition, why don't you just shut up and go into the tasting room and have yourself a free glass of Chardonnay? The choice is up to you, Friend: drink up, or get out; compliments of the house, or go to hell. Take your pick."

Do you see now? Jesus' story of the Laborers in the Vineyard is every bit as much a parable of grace as it is of judgment, and vice versa. It is about a grace that works by raising the dead, not by rewarding the rewardable; and it is about a judgment that falls hard only upon those who object to the indiscriminate catholicity of that arrangement. On the pattern of the Pharisee and the Publican, this parable takes a flock of dead ducks and makes them not only equal to the live wires who worked all day, but a lot happier in the end. If I had to give them a heraldic description, I would say that grace *couchant*—insouciant grace, grace with her hair down, grace sprawled on the chaise lounge with a bottle of champagne—is *sinister* on their coat of arms. And conversely, on the pattern of the Prodigal Son, this parable takes a herd of industrious turtles and whacks them over the head with the bad news that there is only Good News: judgment *rampant,* therefore, stands *dexter* on their device—judgment that lights into everyone with a universal vindication and then sticks its tongue out at anybody who finds that more than he can take.

In the last analysis, though, it is indeed the tiger of judgment rather than the lady of grace that is the main theme of the Laborers in the Vineyard: my purpose in retelling it classroom-style was precisely to dramatize its unique contribution to the judgment side of the equation. When the lord of the vineyard finally laces into the bellyachers—when he finally gives them, in a rhetorical question, the precise reason why judgment falls not on the unacceptable but only on those who will not accept acceptance—he says: "Is your eye evil because I am good?"

It is the evil eye, you see—the *ophthalmós ponērós,* the eye that loves the darkness of its bookkeeper's black ink, the eye that cannot stand the red ink of unsuccess as it appears in the purple light of grace—that is condemned here. Bookkeeping is the only punishable offense in the kingdom of heaven. For in that happy state, the *books* are ignored forever, and there is only the *Book* of life. And in that book, nothing stands against you. There are no debit entries that can keep you out of the clutches of the Love that will not let you go. There is no minimum balance below which the grace that finagles all accounts will cancel your credit. And there is, of course, no need for you to show large amounts of black ink, because the only Auditor before whom you must finally stand is the Lamb—and he has gone deaf, dumb, and blind on the cross. The last may be first and the first last, but that's only for the fun of making the point: everybody is on the payout queue and everybody gets full pay. *Nobody is kicked out who wasn't already in;* the only bruised backsides belong to those who insist on butting themselves into outer darkness.

For if the world could have been saved by bookkeeping, it would have been saved by Moses, not Jesus. The law was just fine. And God gave it a good thousand years or so to see if anyone could pass a test like that. But when nobody did—

when it became perfectly clear that there was "no one who was righteous, not even one" (Rom. 3:10; Ps. 14:1-3), that "both Jews and Gentiles alike were all under the power of sin" (Rom. 3:9) — God gave up on salvation by the books. He cancelled everybody's records in the death of Jesus and rewarded us all, equally and fully, with a new creation in the resurrection of the dead.

And therefore the only adverse judgment that falls on the world falls on those who take their stand on a life God cannot use rather than on the death he can. Only the winners lose, because only the losers can win: the reconciliation simply cannot work any other way. Evil cannot be gotten out of the world by reward and punishment: that just points up the shortage of sheep and turns God into one more score-evening goat. The only way to solve the problem of evil is for God to do what in fact he did: to take it out of the world by taking it into himself—down into the forgettery of Jesus' dead human mind—and to close the books on it forever. That way, the kingdom of heaven is for everybody; hell is reserved only for the idiots who insist on keeping nonexistent records in their heads.

One last comment. Just before Jesus launches into the payout sequence in this parable, he says, *"opsías de genoménēs,* when it was evening, the lord of the vineyard said to his steward. . . ." I have an image for that. On Shelter Island, where I used to live, there is an odd local custom. Every Friday evening, at exactly five minutes of five, the fire siren goes off. For years, I wondered about it. What was the point? They tested the siren every day at noon, so it couldn't be that. I even asked around, but nobody seemed to know a thing about it. Then one day it finally dawned on me: rather than run the risk that the festivity of the rural weekend be delayed even one minute beyond the drudgery of the working week, some gracious soul had decided to proclaim the party from the top of the firehouse—the 4:55 siren was the drinking siren. Miller Time on Shelter Island.

Opsías de genoménēs. Heaven is Miller Time. Heaven is the party in the streaming sunlight of the world's final afternoon.

Heaven is when all the rednecks, and all the wood-butchers, and all the plumbers who never showed up—all the losers who never got anything right and all the winners who just gave up on winning—simply waltz up to the bar of judgment with full pay envelopes and get down to the serious drinking that makes the new creation go round. It is a bash that has happened, that insists upon happening, and that is happening now—and by the sweetness of its cassation, it drowns out all the party poopers in the world.

Heaven, in short, is fun. And if you don't like that, Buster *(hetaíre),* you can just go to . . . well, you'll have to use your imagination.

You'll need it: this is the only bar in town.

CHAPTER FIVE

Resurrection and Judgment

The Raising of Lazarus

Following the Aland chronology, we shift now to the Gospel of John—and to one of the most notable of all Jesus' acted parables, the Raising of Lazarus (John 11:1-44; Aland no. 259). As I mentioned earlier, there was a long period in the twentieth century when John was considered off-limits as a source for legitimate insights into the historical development of Jesus' thought. Things are better now; but since that prejudice still persists here and there, let me make just a few observations about it.

To adapt what Charles Williams once said of the Book of Job: no matter what the critics say about the Fourth Gospel, it is still possible to read it as an English book. I would add that it is not only possible to do so but essential: it is precisely the English version of John's Gospel *as it now stands* (or the Greek original, if you read Greek) that is your best clue to what the Holy Spirit wanted to tell you when he finally said (sometime early in the second century) "Okay, that's a take."

The nonhistorical character of John has been vastly overdone. This is not the place to go into the matter in detail, but for the record, note the following. First, despite certain transpositions (the Cleansing of the Temple in particular), John's chronology is more explicit, and sometimes more reliable, than the synoptics. Second, Jesus' dialogues in John are not just theological flights of fancy; they have about them a realism—

or as Dorothy Sayers put it, a verisimilitude, a dramatic reproducibility—that the synoptics do not often achieve. And third, the passion narrative in John is both chronologically and geographically more verifiable than the accounts in the other three Gospels.

It is simply misleading, therefore, to act as if John is nothing but a theological rhapsody ungrounded by any connection with Jesus' actual ministry. Every one of the Gospels is a theological tract; none of them is the work of a mere chronicler. Their several theologies differ, of course, and John's is admittedly later and "churchier" than the rest. But that is hardly a fatal flaw: Matthew, Mark, and Luke are themselves later than Jesus and every one of them was produced in a context of inescapable churchiness. So say goodbye to the fantasized nonhistorical Jesus of an over-theologized Fourth Gospel. And welcome to the real world of the assorted but unremittingly theological documents by which the New Testament hands us the only Jesus anyone knows beans about.

Accordingly, I make no apology for threading in the Johannine account of the raising of Lazarus here. If its place in the overall Gospel sequence cannot neatly be squared with the differing chronologies of the synoptics, it nonetheless occurs in John at approximately the same point to which Matthew, Mark, and Luke have now brought us, namely, the time just before Palm Sunday. Far more important, though, is the fact that John's account squares perfectly with—no, that is too weak: it actually highlights and gives more convincing evidence for—the *tone,* the subtext, if you will, that the synoptic writers have established for Jesus' words and deeds at this juncture. Because if the other three Gospels show us a Jesus who is working up a head of judgmental steam in anticipation of his approaching death, John gives us a vivid picture of the fire under the boiler, namely, the hostility of the Judean authorities.

In the sections immediately preceding the Raising of Lazarus (John 10:22-42; Aland nos. 257-258), we see Jesus provoking the charge of blasphemy that was to be the basis of his trial and condemnation. The authorities gather around him and ask, "How long will you keep us in suspense? If you are the Christ, tell us plainly." Jesus answers them, "I told you, and you do not believe . . . because you do not belong to my sheep. My sheep hear my voice . . . and no one is able to snatch them out of my Father's hand. I and the Father are one." At those words, the authorities once again try to stone him for blasphemy; but Jesus, after a few more altercations and yet another attempt to arrest him, escapes from their hands, going away across the Jordan. And many came to him, John says, "and believed on him there."

The persistent effort on the part of the Judean authorities to arrest Jesus deserves some comment. It is by no means absent from the synoptics, of course: the plot to destroy (*apollýein*) him is noted in Mark 3:6 and Matt. 12:14, and (after Palm Sunday) in Mark 11:18 and Luke 19:47. But it is in John that the specific word *arrest* (*piázein*, to seize, to catch) is used again and again (John 7:30, 32, 44; 8:20; 10:39; and 11:57). John, accordingly, is the writer who most assiduously develops the subtext of the authorities' plan to proceed against Jesus by the legal device of a charge of blasphemy—and John is the only writer who gives it full play at this point (10:39 and 11:57).

One other note, by now a bit overdue. John's Gospel makes frequent use of the phrase *hoi Ioudaíoi*—which can be translated either as "the Jews" or as "the Judeans." As you may have noticed, I have a number of times taken the liberty of translating it as "the Judean authorities." Granted, translating it as "the Jews" is certainly appropriate at many points in the Fourth Gospel—points at which it is simply explanatory (John 7:2: "the Jews' feast of Tabernacles") or descriptive ("many of the Jews came to comfort Martha and Mary"). But when it takes on a negative connotation—especially when it is used to identify the plotters against Jesus—I find that translation inappropriate, if not downright misleading. I do not think that the author of the Fourth Gospel seriously intends to imply that the Jews, qua Jews, are the villains of his narrative. For one thing, he often uses *hoi Ioudaíoi* in a completely neutral way. He even, on occasion, uses it in a positive way ("Salvation is of the Jews," he has Jesus say in John 4:22; "Many of the Jews . . . believed in him," says the Gospel writer in John 11:45). Jesus was, after all, a Jew: he stood proudly on his own Jewishness; and while he associated scandalously with non-Jews (and even made a non-Jew the hero of his parable of the Good Samaritan), there is no way of turning him into an anti-Semite.

But second, I think that the so-called anti-Semitism of the Fourth Gospel needs a good knock in the head. True enough, there are pejorative uses of *hoi Ioudaíoi* in John; and true enough, vengeful Christians, in shamefully large numbers and for disgracefully long centuries, have gone along with the wickedness. But on any fair reading, John is no more an anti-Semite than Jesus. When he uses *hoi Ioudaíoi* as a pejorative, he is most commonly stigmatizing the Judean authorities, not all Jews; and it is precisely in their status as authorities, not in their status as Jews, that he faults them. If God had become incarnate above the Arctic Circle, the Eskimo authorities would just as readily have tried to do him in; if he had been born in Bethlehem, PA, the Governor of Pennsylvania would have been the one who fudged the law in order to get him. The Messiah we see in the New Testament would have had enemies in high places no matter where he landed. Unfortunately, though, on the principle that "Everybody's got to be somewhere, man," the Judean authorities were the ones whose neighborhood property values were ruined by the incarnate Lord's moving in. Which makes them, as far as I am concerned, more to be pitied than censured. They did God's dirty work for him. It was not nice of God to arrange things that way, but it was at least expectable. The God who tried to murder Moses in an inn (Exod. 4:24)—the God who kept the children of Israel in the wilderness for forty years (Exodus, interminably), the God who blasted Uzzah (2 Sam. 6:7) just for trying to keep the Ark of the Covenant from falling off an oxcart—never advertised himself as the God of Good Manners.

With apologies all around, therefore (too late, too little,

too bad), "the Judean authorities" it is. On to the Raising of Jesus' Dead Friend (John 11:1-44).

The story, which appears only in John, begins by identifying the principal character, Lazarus, as living in Bethany and as being the brother of Mary and Martha. These same two sisters appear in Luke 10:38-42 and again in John 12:1-8. Mary, as it is noted here (John 11:2), is the one who, just before Palm Sunday, anointed the Lord with ointment and wiped his feet with her hair. She is also—if you follow the dubious old practice of scrunching together as many biblical characters as possible—the "woman of the city" who was a sinner (Luke 7:36-50). She is even, if you carry the practice to its extreme, Mary Magdalene.

It is Lazarus, though, who is the most fascinating character. The oddest thing about him—and one of the few scripturally certain things—is that neither here nor elsewhere in the Gospels does he say a word. He appears at a dinner party in John 12:1-8; his name is used by Jesus in Luke 16:19-31 for the beggar in the parable of the Rich Man and Lazarus (an exceedingly odd turn on Jesus' part, because in no other spoken parable does he assign a proper name to one of the characters); and finally, after Lazarus has been raised from the dead, the high priests make plans to kill him all over again "because on account of him, many of the Jews were going off and believing in Jesus" (John 12:9-11). Nowhere, however—not even in the parable in Luke, where "Lazarus" is shown, strikingly, as risen from the dead and resting on the bosom of Abraham—does he have a single line.

But that is not the only oddity. Throughout John 11 the author goes out of his way to establish the uniqueness of the relationship between Lazarus and Jesus. In verse 5, he notes that "Jesus loved Martha and her sister and Lazarus"; in verse 33, he observes that Jesus was angrily upset *(enebrimēsato)* by all the weeping of the mourners; in verse 35, he has Jesus himself weep when he sees the tomb in which Lazarus is buried; in verse 36, the bystanders say "See how he loved him!"; and in verse 38, Jesus approaches the tomb angrily upset again *(em-*

brimômenos). This is a remarkable amount of emotion for a Gospel writer to assign to Jesus. But if you add to it another of John's peculiarities, it becomes more remarkable still.

Only *after* this point in the Gospel does the author begin his strange series of references to an unnamed disciple who reclined on Jesus' breast at the Last Supper—a disciple whom he further identifies as an "other *(állos)* disciple" and also as "that *(ekeínos)* disciple" whom "Jesus loved" (see, for example, John 13:23-25; 18:15-16; 20:2-8; 21:7, 20-23). Indeed, so notable are these references that some commentators have suggested the possibility that this "Beloved Disciple" may actually be Lazarus himself. If that is so, the next to the last verse of the Gospel (John 21:24) takes on a fascinatingly different meaning. The words, "This is the disciple who bore testimony to these things and wrote them down . . . ," become thus a reference to Lazarus who, himself brought back to life by Jesus, becomes the Gospel's principal theological witness to Jesus' own victory as the Resurrection and the Life; and by contrast, the rest of the sentence, namely, ". . . and we know *(oídamen)* that his testimony is true," becomes the voice of the author of the Fourth Gospel.

There is, however, one more singularity about this whole business that I want to note. In some contemporary circles, the suggestion is often made that Jesus and the Beloved Disciple/Lazarus were homosexual lovers; by many contemporary squares, however, that suggestion is met with howls of "Blasphemy!" Let me pour oil on both their waters.

I think the right analogy here is Renaissance art. When the painters of that period depicted, say, the Annunciation, they showed the angel wearing the Sunday-go-to-meeting clothes of their own day: Gabriel looked exactly like some Venetian yuppie. They did not, presumably, think that such a getup was a faithful reproduction of the angel's actual clothing as Mary first saw it: lacking any hard information about first-century styles, they simply imposed their own fashions on the scene and got on with their proper artists' business of trying to show what it meant.

So too with the artistic license involved in making Jesus and the Beloved Disciple lovers. For my money, the inner circles that like that sort of thing are quite within their rights to indulge in it, provided they are doing what the Renaissance painters did: using deliberate anachronism—employing contemporary material to make vivid the historical manifestation of the love of God in Christ Jesus. But I feel they are quite off the mark if they think they can assert with a straight face that a first-century Jewish Messiah candidate, however nonconforming, would actually have been gay. (I feel the same way about the often-dropped heterosexual innuendo that Jesus and Mary Magdalene had something going: as anachronism, run with it; as fact, forget it.) Likewise, the squares are just as right and just as wrong. Jesus was no doubt as straight as any die they want to imagine. Still, they should watch their step: if people who have been beaten up on for lack of straightness want, by a flight of fancy, to make the point that Jesus loves them, too, it ill behooves the rest of us to beat up on them some more.

But enough digression. With peace to everybody's house, back to the story.

When it starts (John 11:1-6), Jesus is not in Bethany but in some other (unidentified) place with his disciples. Mary and Martha send him a message: "Lord, he whom you love is sick." Jesus, however, downplays the news. He tells his disciples that "This sickness is not unto death; it is for the glory of God, so that the Son of God may be glorified by means of it." And he stays right where he is for two days longer. But then he says to the disciples, "Let's go to Judea again." Predictably, they find that foolish: the authorities, they remind him, are still out to get him. But he tells them he'll take his chances: "Lazarus, our friend, has fallen asleep," he says; "but I am going to awake him out of sleep." At first, they misunderstand, thinking that he means Lazarus is enjoying the rest that leads to recovery; but Jesus corrects them, saying plainly that Lazarus is dead (John 11:14). So off they all go.

When Jesus arrives at Bethany, Martha comes out to meet

him, but Mary stays in the house. Martha says to him, "Lord, if you had been here, my brother would not have died." (The reader knows, of course, what Martha doesn't, namely, that Jesus has deliberately stayed away—that he has staged his absence to set up the situation: the author of the Gospel is obviously using every device he knows to stamp this episode as an acted parable.) Martha does indeed go on to add that she knows that whatever Jesus asks from God, God will give him. But Jesus is not interested in what she thinks she knows; he is concerned with what she is willing to believe—concerned, that is, not with her theology but with her faith. So he simply says to her, "Your brother will rise again" (John 11:23).

Time for a halt here. In all likelihood, Mary, Martha, and Lazarus were reared either as Pharisees or under the influence of Pharisaic teaching—as was Jesus himself perhaps. In any case, when Martha responds to Jesus in the very next verse (John 11:24), she sounds exactly as if she is repeating a lesson learned in Pharisee Sunday School: "Oh yes," she says. "I know that. I know he will rise again at the last day." (The notion of a general resurrection at some future date was standard Pharisaic teaching. Not all Jews of the time ascribed to it: the Sadducees, notably, denied the idea outright—see, for example, Mark 12:18-28. At any rate, it is clear from Martha's reply that she for one has bought the idea lock, stock, and barrel.)

What Jesus next says to her, though, goes far beyond anything she or the Pharisees had in mind. "No!" he says to her in effect; "your brother will not rise at the last day, he will rise *now*, because I am the resurrection and the life; he who believes in me, though he die, yet shall he live, and whoever lives and believes in me shall never die." But then he asks her, "Do you believe this?" As I said, he is challenging her to trust in him rather than to rely on her own credence of theological propositions. And Martha comes through: "Yes, Lord," she says, "I believe that you are the Christ, the Son of God, he who is coming into the world."

F. D. Maurice once said that this exchange between Jesus

and Martha depressed him. How sad it is, he observed, that after two thousand years, the church has gotten most Christians only to the point to which the Pharisees got Martha: resurrection in the future, resurrection a week from some Tuesday. Only a handful have ever gotten past that point and made the leap of faith that Jesus got Martha to make: the leap to resurrection *now* — to resurrection as the fundamental mystery of creation finally manifest in his own flesh. And yet that mystery is all over the pages of the New Testament. Not only is it in such epistles as Ephesians and Colossians (see Eph. 2:5-6, for example, or Col. 3:1-4). It is also perfectly plain in the Gospels: *Jesus never meets a corpse that doesn't sit up right on the spot.* Consider. There is the widow of Nain's son (Luke 7:11-17); there is Jairus's daughter (Luke 8:41-56); and there is Lazarus himself. They all rise not because Jesus does a number on them, not because he puts some magical resurrection machinery into gear, but simply because *he has that effect on the dead.* They rise because he is the Resurrection even before he himself rises—because, in other words, he is the grand sacrament, the real presence, of the mystery of a kingdom in which everybody rises.

Back to the text. Martha goes to tell her sister, "The Teacher is here and is calling for you," and Mary comes out quickly to meet him. She too says, "Lord, if you had been here, my brother would not have died." But Jesus is upset *(enebrimḗsato)* and does not reply. (The verb *embrimásthai* is used only a few times in the New Testament; but when it is applied to Jesus, it is used in situations where he is seemingly out of control—where, if I may say so, the power of the mystery that he *is* practically overwhelms the plausible structure of what he is doing. See, for example, Matt. 9:30 and Mark 1:43: the healings that he performs are more extorted from him than done by him. See especially the healing of the woman with the hemorrhage in Luke 8:43-48: the verb *embrimásthai* is not used, but Jesus is so snappish he gives the woman the shakes. In all these instances, Jesus seems less than his own master. He feels [to reach for an analogy] more like a cafeteria counter of

power from which people take what they want than like a res-
taurateur who can give them what he chooses to serve. And it
makes him . . . well, churlish: the Gospels—and John's Gospel
in particular, with its eye for telling detail—show the emotional
price he paid for being the sacrament of the mystery.)

Nevertheless, Jesus plows on: he orders the stone at the
door of the cave-tomb to be taken away. Practical Martha observes (another convincing Johannine detail) that Lazarus has
been dead four days and that by now, in the words of the KJV,
"he stinketh." But Jesus simply reminds her of her promise to
trust, lifts up his eyes, thanks his Father for hearing him, and
then says, with a loud voice, "Lazarus, come out!" "And," the
Gospel says, "the dead man came out, his hands and feet bound
with bandages and his face wrapped in a cloth." Jesus says,
"unbind him, and let him go" (John 11:44). And that, said
John, was that.

For one thing, it was the beginning of the end. In the immediately following passage (John 11:45-53), the chief
priests and the Pharisees gather together in council and Caiaphas the high priest gives it to them straight. They are a
bunch of know-nothings, he tells them. It's time to stop all
the generalized handwringing about what a threat Jesus is and
make some concrete plans to have him killed. He says this,
John adds, not of his own accord but in his official capacity
as high priest and prophet of the people: his lethal dictum, in
other words, is to be taken as nothing less than divinely inspired. The God of Bad Manners rides again: one more semi-
innocent bystander—this time a prudent ecclesiastical politi-
cian just trying to do his job—is suckered into doing the dirty
work of salvation. And so the plot goes into action: "From
that day on," the Gospel says (John 11:53), "they took counsel how to put him to death."

It is all downhill from there. In John 11:54–12:11, Jesus
briefly goes into hiding in a town called Ephraim; he moves
on to Bethany and shows up at a dinner where Mary, Martha,
and Lazarus are present; during the meal, Mary anoints his
feet with some high-priced ointment and Judas Iscariot ob-

jects that if she had sold the whole jar instead, it would have fetched $1200 for the poor (yet another sensible type lights up one of God's exploding cigars); Jesus tells him to get off her back and let her keep it for the day of his burial; a crowd comes—not only to see Jesus but to gawk at Lazarus so recently dead—and as a result of the hubbub, the chief priests decide that Lazarus, too, has to be killed (bystander number three finds himself looking down the divine drain). And then comes Palm Sunday (John 12:12).

But the Raising of Lazarus is more than just the beginning of Jesus' end: I find it to be one of the seminal passages on the meaning of resurrection. Accordingly, I am going to use it as the occasion of a theological interlude I have been waiting for some time now to make. I want you to think about Jesus' insistence to Martha that resurrection is something that happens *now* rather than in the future—that it is a *present* reality rather than just a coming one.

There are two ways of looking at the work of Jesus, two ways of coming at both his incarnation in general and at the several particular manifestations of it in his birth, teaching, miracles, death, resurrection, ascension, and second coming. The first is to go with T. S. Eliot and conceive of it all as the "intersection of the timeless with time." If you do that, you propose to yourself two very different realms—the timeless as opposed to the time-bound, the eternal as opposed to the temporal, or even, if I may stretch the matter a bit, God's "time" as opposed to our "times"—and you thus make the incarnate Lord "the still point of the turning world," the point at which these two realms coincide. Indeed, if you want to put it vividly, as Eliot does, you say that they cross at the Cross—that on Good Friday, God's eternal way of doing business overrides and reconciles our temporal botching of the job. As far as it goes, that is a good enough way of talking about the two— and it is certainly one of the principal ways in which Scripture talks about them. But it is not the only way, and it is not the best way.

It has drawbacks. For if you say only that the incarnation

is *an* action at *a* point in history, you find yourself at odds with some important parts of Scripture. In a number of places, the New Testament insists that the mysterious powers made manifest in the Word's becoming flesh—the absolving grace of Jesus' death, for example, or the reconciling grace of his resurrection, or the vindicating grace of his judgment—cannot be confined to back-then-sometime or back-there-somewhere. Rather, they are right-here-now—and not just in your "now" and mine but in every now that ever was or will be. The mystery does not simply coincide with the world at one point; it coinheres in the world at all points. It is present to all times, not just to the time when Jesus appeared in history; and it is present to all places, not just to the spots where he happened to show up.

Watch the way the New Testament's case for that builds. In Rom. 7:4, Paul says that even while we are alive, we are already "dead to the law by the body of Christ." Jesus' death, you see, is a present reality: besides being a fact of past history, it is a cosmic fact that underlies all history. In Col. 3:3, that fact is buttressed: "You died," Paul says to the historically quite alive Colossians, "and your life is hid with Christ in God." Even before we literally die, therefore, we are already dead in Jesus' death and alive in Jesus' resurrection. But the case is made most clearly in Eph. 2:5-6: since we are thus dead in the mystery of his death, all of us have also, right now, been "made alive together with him" and "raised up together with him" and "seated together with him in the heavenly places." In other words, Scripture shows God in Christ not simply as intersecting history at one moment of time but as being the *eternal contemporary of every moment of time.* What he did in Jesus was neither more nor less than what he had been doing all along.

That makes a considerable difference. If Jesus is only a sacrament of intersection, then the events of the incarnation become saving moments that we have somehow to reach back into history for—that we appropriate chiefly by memory and credence. But if he is the sacrament of concurrence—if what we are invited to believe is that his death and resurrection are the underlying realities of our present existence, if we are called to see those events as manifestations, in a specific time and place, of the mystery that infuses all times and places—then instead of having to *get back to him* by credence, we have only to *reach down to him* in trust and lay hold of the Resurrection and the Life who has been with us all along.

But it is when we come to the subject of what we call his second coming that the theology of concurrence makes the biggest difference of all. For if we think of Jesus simply as coming back for one final intersection of the timeless with time, one last, judgmental stab at tidying up the mess of history, we inevitably conceive of ourselves as pretty much on our own in the meantime. But if we see his judgment, his *krísis* of history, as yet another concurrence with our lives, as one more presence *in every moment of our history,* we are not on our own: his sovereign vindication of all time is with us at every time.

In a fascinating way, Scripture supports this concurrence theology more easily than you might think. The phrase "second coming," despite its popularity, is not the way the New Testament talks about Jesus' appearance in history as judge. The normal term it uses is *parousía*—a word that means simply *presence.* (To be sure, it is easy to read *parousía* as "presence at the end"; but in the light of the "now" passages quoted above, it is just as important to see it as "presence all along.") Indeed, it is precisely in order to stress this present concurrence of judgment with our lives that modern theologians have taken to using another (nonscriptural) Greek work to talk about the *parousía:* its reality, they say, is "proleptic." And what is a *prolépsis*? It is an anticipation in one time of something that will not occur historically until another time. Appropriately enough, they go on to add that this *prolépsis* of judgment is not just a mental anticipation but somehow a real one—an actual, if advance, participation in the final fact. I find that cumbersome, though. Why do mental gymnastics like that when the simpler (and more biblical) notion of concurrence covers the same ground better? Watch.

The mystery manifested in Jesus' death forgives us now

because it is as present now as it was on the cross; the mystery manifested in his resurrection restores us now because it is as present now as it was when he left the tomb; and the mystery manifested in his judgment vindicates us now because it is as present now as it will be when he appears in glory. Those events—the specific "mighty acts of salvation"—were indeed (or indeed will be) sacramental events, real presences of the mystery under historical signs; but like true sacraments, they are not the only instances of its presence. Above all, they are by no means presences of something that wasn't there before. Just as, in communion, Jesus is really present in the bread and wine but cannot be said to have shown up in a gathering from which he was absent (the church that consecrates the eucharistic sign of the body of Christ), so too in the saving acts of his ministry, past or future: the sacramental appearance of Jesus as judge at the last day is indeed a real presence in the courtroom of history, but it is not his arrival in that courtroom for the first time. It is (if you will allow me an extravagance) his popping up from behind the bench and saying, "Surprise! I've been down here on the floor all along, hunting for your indictments; but since I don't seem to find any, go home and have a nice day."

One last theological point while we're on the subject of resurrection and judgment. Perhaps the biggest obstacle to our seeing the judgment of Jesus as the grand sacrament of vindication is our unfortunate preoccupation with the notion of the immortality of the soul. The doctrine is a piece of non-Hebraic philosophical baggage with which we have been stuck ever since the church got out into the wide world of Greek thought. Along with the concomitant idea of "life after death," it has given us almost nothing but trouble: both concepts militate against a serious acceptance of the resurrection of the dead that is the sole basis of judgment.

Consider their effects. If you take the view that there is some imperishable part of you that will go on willy-nilly after you die, you come up with two pieces of bad news. On the one hand, if you think that your immortal soul is all covered with dirty deeds from its trip through life, you are forced to conclude that it will come before Jesus at the last day in very unforgivable shape indeed: the resurrection will give you back your body, but you will still be as guilty as ever in your soul. (Hence the invention of purgatory, that pre-heavenly carwash for souls muddied by traffic on earth.) On the other hand, if you think your immortal soul is squeaky clean and needs only fitting out with a new body to do it justice, you make Jesus practically unnecessary. What do you need him for? All he becomes on that basis is some kind of celestial mechanic who bolts new bodies onto old souls. Worse yet, he becomes an idiotic mechanic who then proceeds to throw away most of his repair jobs because the souls were no good to begin with. His saving work becomes a waste of time *and* eternity.

But if you are willing at least momentarily to suspend your attachment to the idea of a soul that lives after death (I don't suppose you ever will—or even should, maybe—get rid of it altogether), you will finally be able to see the Good News, which is that Jesus came to raise the dead. Not just dead bodies, but dead souls as well. In the beginning, the Word brought creation into being not out of some preexistent glop, but out of nothing; in the end, the incarnate Lord will bring the new creation into being not out of a bunch of used souls but out of death: stone-cold, body-and-soul, nothing-at-all *death*. And therefore all the so-called unbelievers who horrify Christians by saying, "When you're dead, you're dead; there is no life after death," are actually closer to faith in the Gospel than they know: it's the dead who are Jesus' dish, not the living; *nothing* is all he needs—and all he will accept—for the making of anything, old creation or new.

And that, Virginia, is why we look forward with joy to his coming — why we are able to stand with confidence at his *parousía*. By the power of the Resurrection who works in our total death, none of our garbage goes with us into the new creation. Lose your immortal soul, then, and you'll get an everlasting life that's worth living.

CHAPTER SIX

The Onset of the Hurricane

The Final Prediction of the Passion; James and John;
Blind Bartimaeus; Zacchaeus; the Parable of the Coins

Back now to the synoptic Gospels for the first of the full-fledged parables of judgment: the parable (Aland no. 266) of the Coins (Luke 19:11-27), or of the Talents (Matt. 25:14-30). However, since Aland's *Synopsis* lists four transitional episodes between the point at which we just left John's Gospel (Aland no. 261) and the point at which Jesus tells this parable, let me devote a few paragraphs to each of them in order to set the stage.

In Aland no. 262 (Matt. 20:17-19; Mark 10:32-34; Luke 18:31-34), Jesus makes the final prediction of his approaching passion and death. Mark's version is the most vivid: Jesus and his followers are on the road to Jerusalem and Jesus is walking on ahead of them all by himself. They are "amazed" *(ethambounto)*, Mark says; and they are "afraid" *(ephobounto)*. Clearly, everyone in Jesus' company senses that something dire is just down the road; and sure enough, taking the twelve aside, he repeats for the third time his prophecy of the death and resurrection of the "Son of man." (I know, Virginia: some people say he wasn't talking about himself in any of these predictions—that it is only a later ecclesiastical tradition that says Jesus and the Son of man are one and the same. What do I think about that? I find it hard to square with Mark: if Jesus was just rattling on about some third party's demise, why was

73

he giving off vibes that scared the living daylights out of his followers? And as far as "ecclesiastical tradition" is concerned, his followers were just as much the church as any group that came later. Their consternation suggests to me that this tradition, if that's what you want to call it, started rather early—right on the Gospel spot, in fact, and precisely because Jesus himself caused it to start there.)

In any case, what we have in all three Gospel accounts of this prediction is the same thing we just had in John: the synoptic writers are cranking up the heat of passion and death before launching into the events of Holy Week, and they are doing so to give the proper introduction to Jesus' "hot" parables of judgment. As I said, Jesus is not on a stroll here through the groves of academe. He is on his way to the dreadful *éxodos* spoken of by Moses and Elijah at the transfiguration and he is not cool about it: in addition to foreseeing the pain, he knows full well that practically nobody—hardly any of his disciples and certainly none of his fellow countrymen—will be able to make head or tail of it.

His prescience is amply vindicated by what happens next in Matt. 20:20-28 and Mark 10:35-45 (Aland no. 263). James and John, if you follow Mark (or their mother speaking for them, if you follow Matthew), come to Jesus and ask that they be granted the privilege of sitting on his right hand and on his left in glory. These lines are so bizarre that any scriptwriter who tried to get away with them would be told to go back and write something that didn't completely ignore the scene before. It simply strains credulity to think that Jesus' disciples, having just heard him predict his death, could so completely gloss over what he said and go blathering on about heavenly seating arrangements.

But if you understand the disciples as Jesus did—if you see them in the hot light of his certainty that they do not understand a thing about what he is really doing—the bizarreness of their request makes perfectly good dramatic sense. They are amazed and they are afraid. They are out of their depth completely. So, just as Peter at the transfiguration burst out with the first plausible, let's-get-hold-of-ourselves idea that came into his head ("Let's make three tents . . ."), James and John put as much distance as they can between themselves and the awful Main Subject. "Let's talk about something more cheerful," they say, hoping perhaps to cheer up Jesus as well in the process; "let's talk about what it will be like when this is all over." Jesus, however, will not be jollied. He asks them if they are able to drink the cup that he drinks, or to be baptized with the baptism with which he is baptized. And when, predictably, they say, "Sure," he lets out a long, resigned breath and says "O . . . kay; because that will be exactly what you'll get. I'm into death and resurrection here, and that's all I'm into. The business of who gets what seats is not my job."

The other ten, of course, are no better than James and John: hearing Jesus' words only as a rebuke to a cheeky request, they become indignant at the two brothers. But Jesus ignores their dim-wittedness too and presses on with the Main Subject. "Forget all this nonsense about precedence," he tells them; "that's not what I called you for. If any of you wants to be great, he's going to have to be servant of all; and if any of you wants to be first, he's going to have to be slave of all. *For the Son of man came not to be served but to serve, and to give his life as a ransom for many.*" Nothing, you see—not even rampant incomprehension from his disciples—can get Jesus off his preoccupation with death.

The passage that follows next (Matt. 20:29-34 and parallels; Aland no. 264) may seem to be a digression, but it is not. Since all three of the synoptics agree in placing a healing of the blind at this very point, the presumption is either that Jesus did one here, or that the writers thought it fit here, or both. At any rate, whether it was the restoring of sight to just one man (Mark and Luke) or to two (Matthew), it is an acted parable of the blindness of everyone to Jesus' real work. Consider. The crowd around him rebukes the blind beggar: the important Rabbi, they seem to think, must not be exposed to this loser, especially when they are trying so resolutely to soft-pedal the Rabbi's own preoccupation with losing. But Jesus heals blind Bartimaeus anyway (the name occurs in Mark), and at the end he says, "Go your way; your faith has saved you." And, as all three synoptic writers report, "immediately he received his sight" and followed Jesus. In other words, the accounts are making the same point Jesus made with Martha: he is not interested in what those around him think they know, only in what they can be led to believe. They will be saved not by following their own dim ideas about how the kingdom ought to work but by coming to him blindly in the mystery of his death and following him through it into the healing of his resurrection.

The last episode before the parable of the Coins occurs as Jesus nears Jerusalem and is passing through Jericho: in Luke 19:1-10 (Aland no. 265), he meets a man named Zacchaeus who is "a chief tax collector, and rich." The story is not only charming; it is a fascinating excursus on judgment as well. Zacchaeus, for all his wealth, has two problems. Not only does everyone hate him for being a publican, a tax farmer in the employ of the Romans; they also give him bad marks for being ridiculously short: five-foot-two, maybe, or four-foot-eleven. So as Jesus passes by, Zacchaeus is out of luck twice. The crowd won't let him up front because he is a traitor to his people, and his height makes it impossible for him to see anything from down in back. Zacchaeus, however, is not fazed: he runs on ahead and climbs up into a sycamore tree for a better view of the parade. But when the entourage reaches his tree, he gets a surprise: Jesus looks at him and says, "Zacchaeus, hurry up and get down out of there; I'm having dinner with you today."

Zacchaeus is thrilled, of course, but the crowd is appalled: Jesus, they mutter, is going to be the guest of a man who is a sinner! Nevertheless, Jesus goes right on in. But just as he settles down for a nice, relaxed meal, Zacchaeus stands up and launches into a during-dinner speech. "Look, Lord," he says, trying to dispel his universally bad press; "I give half of what I have to the poor, and if I have given anyone a raw deal, I make it up to him four times over."

Time out. When I expounded the parable of the Pharisee and the Publican in *The Parables of Grace*, I said that everybody has a problem with it. Sure, we rejoice that the smarmily good Pharisee is condemned and that the publican—who does nothing more than admit he is worthless—"goes down to his house justified rather than the other." But I also noted that if we are honest, we don't like that very much. I maintained that if we were to imagine a sequel to the parable in which we sent the publican back to the temple one week later, we would almost certainly feel obliged to send him back with some improvement in his life to lay before God—that we would, in short, be tempted to send him back with what amounts to the Pharisee's speech in his pocket.

Do you see now what the acted parable of Zacchaeus is all about? It is precisely a publican making the Pharisee's speech—a loser who thinks that, thank God and his better instincts, he has gotten over his losing behavior and become a twenty-four karat winner. And what does Jesus say to him? He says something straight off the wall: with no intervening explanation, Jesus announces, "Today salvation has come to this house, since he also is a son of Abraham. For the Son of man came to seek and to save the lost." In other words, Jesus brings Zacchaeus back down to the only ground on which he can possibly stand and receive a favorable judgment: the ground of the last, the lost, the least, the little, and the dead.

As to why that odd bit about "a son of Abraham" is in there, I frankly have no good idea. Maybe it means that it is not Zacchaeus's list of good deeds that saves him but simply his status as one more loser in the long history of God's preference for losers—for types like over-the-hill Abraham, under-the-gun Moses, down-the-drain Jeremiah, or for that matter the entire out-of-luck nation he clutched to his bosom as his chosen people. Then again, maybe it doesn't. But the bit about "seeking and saving the lost" is crystal clear: Jesus is uttering a judgment here, and he is uttering it on the only basis he will allow. He will not judge the cluttered business of our lives, because on that basis none of us will be anything but condemned. He will judge us only as he raises us, reconciled and restored, out of the uncluttered nothingness of our death.

And so you come to the final twist in this acted-out version of the Pharisee and the Publican. In the spoken parable, both characters go down from the temple to their houses, the one condemned for taking his stand on a life that cannot bear judgment, the other justified for taking his stand on a death that can. In this acted parable, however, *the Temple himself*— the Lord who dies and rises, the One who in John 2:19 said, "Destroy this Temple [his body] and I will raise it up in three days"—*comes to Zacchaeus's house and brings salvation.* Just because Jesus is the Resurrection and the Life—just because he has *that effect* on the dead—and just because Zacchaeus is standing there as a solid brass dead duck, Jesus raises him up uncondemned. "Look, Zacchaeus," he says in effect, "just bag it, will you? I have no use for all this chin music about your life. I'm on my way to make the death you're avoiding safe— to make it the only ticket anyone will ever need. Sit down and eat up. Let's just have a quiet dinner before I go down into the silence and solve your problem."

With all of that by way of preface, we turn now to the parable of the Coins/Talents. In Luke's Gospel, this story occurs right after the episode with Zacchaeus (Luke 19:1-10) and right before Palm Sunday (19:28-44). In Matthew, however, the material appears in a somewhat different form and in another place: he presents it as the parable of the Talents and he puts it in at Matt. 25:14-30, just before the beginning of the passion narrative. I am tempted, of course, to go with the Lukan version at this point not only because it is in strict sequence with what we have just been reading but also because it has a number of fascinating convolutions. Nevertheless, since Matthew, too, makes unique contributions to the story, I think it best to expound the parable by reading back and forth between the two versions, especially in view of the possibility that their differences may not be due to the authors, but to Jesus himself: he may perfectly well have told this story twice and, like an entertainer who ad-libs on his own material, put in just these variations.

Let us begin with Luke. "As they heard these things," the

Gospel says (19:11), "Jesus proceeded to tell a parable. . . ." Initial questions: Where is Jesus when he tells this parable; who are "they"; and what "things" is Luke talking about? Answers: Jesus is still in Zacchaeus's house, or else he is continuing on the road to Jerusalem; "they" are at least a portion of the same group that heard him in Zacchaeus's house; and the "things" are either what he said to Zacchaeus or even, possibly, all the things he said from Luke 18:31 on. But then Luke continues his introduction to the parable by giving two reasons why Jesus tells it. The first is, "because he was near to Jerusalem," and the second, "because they supposed that the kingdom of God was to appear immediately." The next question, therefore: What is Luke trying to indicate by this unusually explanatory preface? Answer (I think): he is suggesting that the behavior of Jesus just prior to this point—his foreboding manner and especially his repeated use of the phrase "the Son of man"—has made everyone around him think of things like the coming of the kingdom and the judgment of the world. They have all, Luke implies, leapt straight to one of the human race's favorite subjects: eschatology. But he also wants to indicate that Jesus is unhappy with such a facile leap. For one thing, Jesus knows that *for now* the manifestation of the mystery will not be anything like what they expect: the kingdom will be revealed by way of his death and resurrection, not by way of some direct, razzle-dazzle intervention in the affairs of the world. It will, in short, be paradoxical rather than plausible. For another thing though, Jesus feels a need to correct their equally erroneous notion of what the coming of the kingdom means *for then*—for the future. He wants to challenge their customary thinking about the subject of judgment, because even the judgment, he is convinced, will be nothing like what they have in mind.

For what they expect on that count is something equally plausible: a coming of the Son of man to knock heads and settle scores, to reward the good and punish the wicked by simple, right-handed justice. Note here, incidentally, that this is precisely what the phrase "Son of man," in its then current meaning, would have led them to think. Even though I have said that I think Jesus did indeed identify himself with "the Christ" (the Messiah) and "the Son of man" (reinterpreting both concepts mightily in the process), I nevertheless think it important to remember that his followers would not necessarily have equated those two figures either with Jesus or with each other. On the one hand, "the Christ," as far as they were concerned, was to be God's chosen agent for the bringing in of the kingdom; on the other hand, "the Son of man" was to be an eschatological figure who would preside over the last judgment. In any case, since Jesus has, by his words and behavior, put both the kingdom and the judgment on the table, as it were, Luke clearly wants us to bear both subjects in mind as we read the parable that now unfolds in all its left-handed, implausible detail.

"A nobleman went into a far country," Jesus begins, "to receive kingly power and then return." Let me interrupt myself right at the start and alert you to a procedural device I have decided to use. Even though I think it is generally a poor idea to make point-for-point theological identifications of the details of Jesus' parables, I am going to make an exception here: after certain words or phrases in Luke's text, I shall use square brackets [   ] to flag what I consider to be the likely theological referents of the several elements in this parable. I shall make these insertions without comment as I go along; but by the end of my exposition, I think you will find that they have become quite understandable. Accordingly, let me repeat the parable's opening line quoted above, this time putting in the theological flags I want to wave at you.

"A nobleman (*eugenēs,* well-born) [this nobleman is the Christ-figure of the parable, corresponding to Jesus, the *monogenēs,* the only begotten of God] went into a far country [death] to receive kingly power [to rise from the dead] and then return [to appear to his disciples after the resurrection, and also to sit in universal judgment at the *parousía*]. Calling ten of his servants, he gave them ten *mnas,* ten coins [since each servant received one coin, this stands for every human being's equal reception of the sovereign grace of resurrection from the dead]. And he said to them, 'Trade *(pragmateúsasthe)* with these till I come.'"

Matthew, who begins the parable only at this point—and without anything corresponding to Luke's preface—says there were just three servants; furthermore, instead of having them receive equal shares, he assigns to the first, five talents *(tálanta),* to the second, two, and to the third, one. Luke, however, having established the number of servants as ten, seemingly distracts our attention from them by inserting a strange paragraph about the nobleman's other subjects. He tells us, in Luke 19:14: "But his citizens hated him [the paradox of going away into death is profoundly repugnant to everyone: to the disciples, to the authorities, to the crowds, to us], and they sent representatives after him with the message, 'We do not want this man to reign over us' [the paradox is also radically unacceptable]."

But there are still more differences at this point between the two versions of the parable. At Matt. 25:16, on the one hand, we find a brief, anticipatory summary of what the servants did with their several talents—the information that will be repeated later in the "judgment" section of the story. Luke, on the other hand, omits this duplication and goes straight to the day of reckoning (Luke 19:15): "When the nobleman returned, having received kingly power [when, that is, Jesus returns in both the resurrection and the *parousía*], he commanded that these servants to whom he had given the money be called to him in order that he might know what they had gained by trading [that is, by accepting—or in the case of the 'wicked,' not accepting—the freely given acceptance by grace]." The subtle difference between the Matthean and the Lukan accounts, therefore, now begins to be manifest. Luke's version just quoted leaves open the possibility of interpreting the nobleman's return as either the resurrection or the *parousía*—even, perhaps, of interpreting the *parousía* as a present as well as a future fact. Matthew, however, tilts very much toward a last-day, last-judgment interpretation: he has Jesus say, "Now *after a long time* the master of those servants came and settled accounts with them."

Nevertheless, the two versions of the parable proceed in substantial agreement from here on. Matthew's first servant comes and reports that his five talents have earned him five more; Luke's, that his one coin has made him ten. Incidentally, the *mna,* or mina, was a coin worth about 1/60th of a *tálanton* — or, to put it in terms of smaller denominations, worth about 100 *denarii,* a *denarius* being the equivalent of a day's pay. You may work out the modern equivalents of the various sums if you like; I find something else far more interesting. In Matthew, the original grants to the servants are all different, but the increments earned are the same as the grants: five on top of five; two on top of two. In Luke, however, the grants are the same (one coin for each), but the increments are all different. Luke, it seems, is taking a page from Mark's version of the parable of the Sower (where the seed sown is Grace himself; the Word incarnate in Jesus). In that account, an equal sowing results, even on uniformly good ground, in an unequal harvest: some thirty-, some sixty-, some a hundredfold. Even though Luke omits this note of diversity of yield from his own account of the Sower, he apparently feels obliged to put it in here (because, perhaps, he finds it congruent with the *sovereignty of grace over judgment* that is the unique feature of his version of the parable).

At any rate, both Luke and Matthew next bring on the second servant and have him report: Luke's man has made five coins with his one; Matthew's, two talents with his two. And in the case of both the master in Matthew and the nobleman in Luke, the response is a judgment of approval. "Well done, good and faithful *(pistós)* servant," says the master (Matt. 25:21); "you have been faithful over a little *(epí olíga),* I will set you over much; enter into the joy of your master." The same note is struck in Luke 19:17: "Well done, good servant! Because you have been faithful *(pistós)* over a very little *(en elachístō,* in the least), you shall have authority over ten cities [Jesus works in leastness, littleness, lastness, lostness, and

death: those, plus *faith in him,* are the only things his resur-
recting grace passes judgment on; the good works and good
results in this parable are praised only as sacraments, effective
signs of the fidelity-in-littleness that the story is really about]."

But then comes the crucial point of the parable: the judgment issued against the servant who acts not out of faith but
out of prudence (just as we do when we fearfully try to deal
with God on the basis of what we *think he is like* rather than
on the basis of what we *trust him to be* in Jesus). Up comes
the weasel himself: "Oh Sir," he says (I conflate the accounts),
"here is your coin, which I have kept bright and shiny in a
handkerchief in my bureau drawer. Because, you see, I was
afraid. I *know* you. You are a hard (Matthew: *sklērós;* Luke:
austērós) man. I know you grab everything, even if it doesn't
belong to you. So I thought to myself, 'Watch your step, Arthur; if he keeps track of every penny everywhere like that,
even when it's not his, just think how mad he could get if you
should happen to lose something that *was* his.' And so, Sir,
here I am and here's your money, in full and on time. Tell me
I'm a good boy."

"No!" roars the nobleman, twice as angry as anything Arthur ever imagined. "I will judge *(krinō)* you out of your own
mouth. You are not a good boy. You are not even a good weasel.
If you knew *(ḗdeis)* I was such a tough customer, why didn't
you at least put my money into a savings account? What? You
thought I'd be mad at a measly 4 1/2 percent? You think I'm
not madder at zero percent? But you know something? That's
not really what I'm mad about. Look, Arthur. I invited you
into a fiduciary relationship with me. That's *fiduciary,* f-i-d: as
in *fides* in Latin—and as in *pístis* in Greek, which is the language this story will end up in—and as in *faith,* in plain English. I didn't ask you to make money, I asked you to do business—that's *pragmateúsasthai,* remember?—to exercise a little
pragmatic trust that I meant you well and that I wouldn't mind
if you took some risks with my gift of a lifetime. But what did
you do? You decided you had to be more afraid of me than of
the risks. *You* decided. You played it safe because of some im-

aginary fear. And so now, instead of having gotten yourself a nice new life as mayor of at least a small city, you have only the crummy little excuse for a life you started with. As a matter of fact, Arthur, you haven't even got that, because you know what I'm going to do? I'm going to take what I gave you and just for fun [to show the outrageousness of grace, as in the Laborers in the Vineyard] I'm going to give it to that guy over there who already has more than he knows what to do with. And you know why I'm going to do that? First of all, to remind everybody that when I give you a gift [grace, forgiveness], I expect you to do business with it, to keep it moving [to forgive others as you are forgiven—see the Lord's Prayer], not just to keep it to yourself in some damned napkin [some low-risk spiritual life in which you neither sin much nor love much—see Luke 7:36-50]. But second, I'm going to give him your gift to show everybody that I never really cared about results anyway [the Laborers in the Vineyard again—the gift of grace is not a reward for hard work or good behavior, it is a lark, a joke, a hilariously inequitable largesse: it is, in a word, a *gift*]. Don't you see, Arthur? It's all a game. All that matters is that you play at all, not that you play well or badly. You could have earned a million with the money I gave you, or you could have earned two cents. You could even have blown it on the horses for all I care: at least that way you would have been a gambler after my own heart. But when you crawl in here and insult me—*me,* Mr. Risk Himself [Jesus the vindicating judge] —by telling me you decided that I couldn't be trusted enough for you to gamble on a two-bit loss, that I was some legalistic type who went only by the books [judgment by law instead of grace], well. . . ."

The two accounts of this tirade diverge here; so let me, in the style of John Fowles, give you two endings to it. Matthew 25:30 first:

". . . you just listen, you little creep," the master roars on. "If you can't live with my kind of acceptance—which is that I can accept absolutely everything except distrust in my acceptance—you can get the hell out of here. Boys! Show Arthur

84

the door. I know it's dark out there, but what does he care? He's got a weasely little concept of me in his weasely little mind and he thinks that if he chews on it long enough, it will turn into a bright idea. But it never will, so get rid of him. Let him wear out his weasely little teeth gnawing on it forever."

If, however, you find that a bit strong for your stomach— if you are hoping that blessed Luke, the patron saint of heal-ing grace, will come through with something softer—don't hold your breath. The outrage of law violated is nothing com-pared to the white-hot fury of grace spurned. Watch the Lukan ending (Luke 19:27):

". . . Hey!" says the nobleman [the dead and risen Jesus], "I've got an idea. Instead of just kicking Arthur the hell out of here, why don't we make a real hell of this and give him some company in his misery? You remember all those other types, Boys? All the ones who were so mad at me for going into the far country [Jesus' death] and for receiving kingly power [Jesus' resurrection]? The ones who wouldn't trust me and even tried to overthrow my government [Jesus' easy yoke and light burden, his gracious rule of grace beyond the rules] . . . well, drag them in here and kill them all in front of me. Not only will it do the universe a favor to get rid of such a bunch of wet blankets; it will do them a favor too. They're dead al-ready and don't know it: the second death shouldn't bother them at all. Why, they'll hardly even. . . ."

See? I told you it would be worse. So just to cheer you up, I will write my own ending to the Lukan ending. Maybe you won't be happy with this one either (some people are hard to please, even with good news); but at least you won't be able to say I didn't try. So here goes nothing, taking it from "the second death" just before we left off:

". . . the second death shouldn't bother them at all. Why, they'll hardly even . . ." But suddenly the nobleman brightens. "Come to think of it," he says, "that gives me an idea. If death and faith are all I need to make everybody a mayor, what dif-ference does it make whether it's first death or second death? Maybe if I could figure out some way of getting them to trust me even in *that* . . ." But then, just as suddenly, he frowns: "I don't know, though. It'd be a tough nut to crack [the theologians would never sit still for a God who wants to be a barefaced universalist]. . . still, it's an idea; so . . . [and thus in the end, God formulates plan Z, the ultimate eschatological cureall: he doesn't ask the theologians' permission; he goes ahead and does it anyway, offering *them* the second death just in case they need a fallback position to guarantee the eternity of hell]."

I thank you for your patience with me through this long exercise in doing three or four things at once. Let me now, with plain words and as straight a face as I can manage, sum up the parable of the Coins/Talents.

It is about the "one thing necessary" (see Luke 10:42): the response of trust, of faith in Jesus' free acceptance of us by the grace of his death and resurrection. It is, in other words, about a faithful, Mary-like waiting upon Jesus himself as the embodiment of the mystery—and about the danger of substituting some prudent, fretful, Martha-like business of our own for that waiting. It is not at all about the rewarding of good works or the punishment of evil ones. The servants who gained varying amounts by their faithful trading gained them by the luck of the draw, not by (at least in Luke) the proportionate effectiveness of the original grant (it was the same in all cases), and probably not even by any proportionate exertions of their own (at any rate, we are told of none). And the servant who was cast out was not guilty of doing any substantive evil thing (the money he was given was returned in full). The parable, therefore, declares that the only thing that is to be examined at the judgment is faith, not good deeds; and it declares that the only thing that can deprive us of the favorable judgment already passed upon us by Jesus is our unfaith in his gracious passing of it (see, once again, John 3:16ff.; chapter 2, above).

One last point. The precise form that the condemned servant's unfaith took was the hiding of the coin "in a napkin." What that says to me is that if we keep Jesus only as a memento—or better said, if we keep the sacramentalities by which he disclosed the mystery only as events to be remembered or as ideas and doctrines to be kept intact—we put ourselves out of the reach of his reconciliation. Because just as the nobleman was present to his servants in and through the coins even in his apparent absence from them, so Jesus is present to us *now* and he calls us to faith in him *now*. Jesus our Death is with us now; Jesus our Resurrection is with us now; and Jesus our Vindicating Judge is with us now—if only now we will *believe*. Not *think*, because all we will ever think of on our own is the godawful God we have made in the image of our worst fears. Not *ratiocinate*, because drawing logical conclusions from our habitual, dreadful premises will only make us more fearful still. And not *reason* and not *speculate* and not *theologize*; just *trust*. Just, "Yes, Jesus. Thank you."

After that, of course, we can intellectualize ourselves silly. After the good servants had been faithful, they were free to write MBA theses on sound management techniques if that sort of thing appealed to them. But not before. Which is why—to end on a suitably theological note, having made my prior act of faith—the "quest for the historical Jesus" is a crashing mistake. We are not in the business of going back in time to look for some intellectually creditable character whom we can then decide to trust. All that ever accomplishes is to fob off on Jesus the trendy qualities we have decided will pass muster: he becomes a good example, or a wise guru, or an ethical authority —none of which could ever even save you a seat on the subway, let alone redeem a sinful world. We are in the business not of going back to him in time but of going down to him in faith —of taking the whole weird Jesus we now find in the Scriptures, and the whole, even weirder Jesus we now have to put up with in the church, and the whole, quintessentially weird Jesus now present to us in everything, nice or not nice—and of laying hold, in him, of the salvation we already have, *now*.

For if we do that, we will have done the only business that we, or the servants in the parable, ever had to do in the first place: trust the Lord in his grace and let the results be whatever we can manage to make them. Good, bad, or indifferent, we are home free, just for the believing.

CHAPTER SEVEN

God's Action in History

Palm Sunday; the Weeping over Jerusalem;
the Cleansing of the Temple; the Cursing of the Fig Tree

We come now at last to Palm Sunday, and to the succeeding days of Jesus' final ministry in Jerusalem. At the beginning of this book, I gave you some statistics to show how disproportionate a space the canonical Gospels give to the passion narrative strictly so called, that is, to the events from the Last Supper on Thursday to Jesus' Death on Friday. But if you work out the percentages of space they give to the extended passion narrative—to the events from Palm Sunday to the Ascension (a period of a month and a half at the most)—the disproportion is even more evident. Here are the figures: in Matthew, this climactic sequence occupies 29 percent of the book; in Mark, 38 percent; in Luke, 21 percent; and in John, 43 percent.

Startling as those figures are, though, I find another fact even more remarkable at this point: Jesus begins the week of his passion and death with a sustained series—no, that is not strong enough—with a catena, a chain of *acted parables*. Palm Sunday (Aland no. 269) is followed immediately by his Weeping over Jerusalem, his Cleansing of the Temple, and his Cursing of the Fig Tree (Aland nos. 270-275). I want, therefore, to make a pause here and spend a little time on the theological significance of the concept of the acted parable.

As I have used the phrase so far, its meaning is clear

enough: an acted parable is an episode in Jesus' ministry in which his deeds rather than his words carry the freight of what he is trying to communicate. His spoken parables are fictions; our response to them in faith is based solely on *his having made them up,* not on there having been, say, an actual good Samaritan, or a real nobleman who gave money to his servants. But his acted parables are historical deeds; in their case, our faith-response depends on *his personally having done them*—so much so, that if we take the view that they are simply stories about him concocted by others, they lose the taproot of their authority. To put it differently, Jesus is the star of the drama of salvation; if these bits of stage business that we respond to as communications without words are only creative fictions from the fertile minds of his reviewers, they hardly deserve the kind of attention the Gospels invite us to give them. Accordingly, their historicity—their authenticity as part of the original performance—becomes a consideration of central importance, not just a frill that can be dismissed as a matter of indifference. That historical significance is just what I propose to enlarge upon in this theological excursus. I am going to suggest that Jesus' acted parables are a key to understanding the fundamental nature of the entire play. I shall try to help you see that it is not only the Triumphal Entry or the Cleansing of the Temple that are parabolic deeds; all of the weightier actions of the Savior are acted parables, too: the Crucifixion, the Resurrection, the Ascension, the Second Coming—even, if you will, all of his anticipatory, "antityping" acts in the Old Testament (more on the notion of antitypes in a little while).

My reason for taking this tack is simple. For most of this century, biblical criticism has been caught over the barrel of whether Jesus' mighty acts were historical events or just subsequent mythologizings designed to make vivid the "faith-experience" of the early church—over the question, in plain English, of whether they were fact or fiction. It seems to me that the concept of the acted parable offers a way of converting this devitalizing "either/or" into a robust "both/and" that allows us to posit not only the historicity of, say, the Resurrection or the Ascension but the theological significance as well. It enables us to say that Jesus did indeed do the things the Scriptures say he did; but it also makes it possible to see those historical actions as parables, as acted-out stories—even, if you will, as *mythic* (not, please note, mythical) events. It makes them, in short, not *mere* anything: neither mere history stuck back there in time somewhere, nor mere fabrications of faith floating unmoored in a nonhistorical sea of significance. They are all, *then* and *now,* history and myth at once.

But since this both/and approach can itself be formulated in two ways—since you can see divine revelation by means of authentic historical occurrences in two different, even contradictory, lights—I propose to illustrate the problem for you by resorting to the classroom teacher's device of going to the blackboard. Watch closely, therefore. The first line I shall draw will represent the entire history of the world (or even the universe, if you like) from start to finish, from the moment of creation to the end of time, from *a* to *z:*

a ————————————————————————— z
History

Now then. The question arises: how, on this analogy, shall we depict the mighty acts of salvation? The first (and less than adequate) answer is easy. Since God, the Alpha and the Omega, the A and Ω, is up there above history, I shall draw a series of descending lines to represent his several comings down—his interventions in history, his intersections with history. These will be (to select a small but significant sample) the Creation, the Call of Abraham, the Ministry of Moses, the Birth of Jesus, the Crucifixion, the Resurrection, the Ascension, and the Second Coming. My illustration will now look like that on the following page.

Things are going swimmingly. Not only is God really acting in history; we ourselves are doing justice to the language of the Nicene Creed: "*he came down from heaven,* and became incarnate, etc.*"

But things are also starting to sink. The picture we have

90

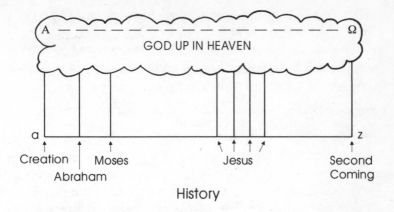

History

drawn looks like nothing so much as a divine sewing machine, with the needle coming down at various points (though not at others) and tacking history to God. It is salvation as the divine basting stitch. Even if the thread holds, there is more of creation unsewn to its Maker and Redeemer than there is sewn. God's mighty acts have become just so many discrete *transactions,* just so many *jobs done*—and done, in fact, only at specific points. Our drawing, in short, is good as far as historicity is concerned (the points at which the needle enters the cloth of the world are indeed real times and places, real events); but it is not so good as far as the mystery of God's presence to all of history is concerned (the spaces between the needle thrusts still constitute most of the world's actual days and years).

Let me show you, therefore, another way of drawing the picture. This time, I shall represent the whole of history, from *a* to *z,* as a body of water:

History

But now, let me posit God not as a divine tailor in heaven sending down an interventionist needle from time to time but as a divine iceberg present under all of time. On that analogy, one-tenth of his presence to history will be visible above the surface of its waters and nine-tenths will be invisible below the

91

surface, *but his presence out of sight will be just as much a part of history as his presence in broad daylight.* Or to put it the other way around, all of history will thus be intimately and immediately present to the mystery of his entire work and being. Let me draw the mystery part first:

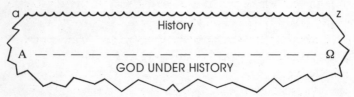

Do you see? If we now proceed to sketch in the mighty acts of God in history, we will not show him as coming down from somewhere else and intervening in a process from which he was absent; we will instead represent his appearances above the surface of history—his revelations of the mystery—as outcroppings, as emergences into plain sight of the tips of the one, continuous iceberg under all of history. Thus, when we draw in our same previous series of mighty acts, they become not *forays into history* of an alien presence from above but *outcroppings within history* of an abiding presence from below.

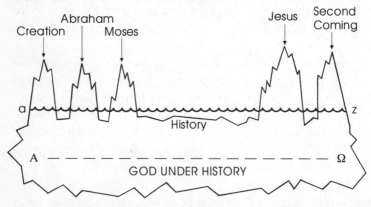

That's better. Although it started out sinkingly—with God down there in the drink out of sight—it ends up going more swimmingly than the first illustration: it does justice to the principle of sacramentality I have been stressing all along in this book. The divine acts in history are not just occasional interventions of a reality that wasn't present before; they are precisely acted parables—sacraments, if you will, real presences—of a reality that was there all along. Like Jesus' presence in the Holy Communion on a Sunday morning, they are real events in real times and places. But like that same presence, they are not simply arrivals upon a scene from which he was absent; they are manifestations, at a specific point, of a mystery that was never absent at any point.

Better yet, the *whole* of the mystery that thus underlies creation is present every time one of those sacramental outcroppings of the mystery occurs. It is not, for example, that the mystery of the Creation occurs only at the beginning, to be superseded later on by the mystery of the Passover and then by the mystery of the Cross, the mystery of the Resurrection from the dead, and the mystery of the Judgment at the End. It is that those several manifestations are outcroppings of a single, age-long mystery of Creation-Call-Passover-Redemption-Resurrection-Judgment that is fully present in every one of them. Just as each upthrusting of the iceberg is one and the same iceberg in a visible aspect, so each upthrusting of the mystery is a visible aspect of one and the same mystery. The Word who becomes incarnate in Jesus is the same Word who spoke the world into being from the start. The Lamb slain on Calvary is the same Paschal Lamb whose blood kept the angel of death from the Jews in Egypt. And the Judge who comes at the end is none other than the gracious, vindicating Savior who rose from the dead—and who, in fact, is present to the whole of history, whether at the raising up of Adam from the dust, or of Isaac from the altar of sacrifice, or of the Jews from the Babylonian captivity, or of Lazarus from the tomb.

As you may be aware, this unifying, Jesus-is-everywhere-in-the-Bible method of interpreting the history of salvation has been around for a long time. If you have ever looked at the running page headings printed in some editions of the King James Bible, you will recall that the compilers of that version felt quite free to read Christ into the Old Testament. It was not just that they found *prophecies* of him in the text (see, for example, the heading over Isa. 28: "Christ, the sure foundation, promised"); they also found *presences* of him (see the heading over Isa. 49: "Christ sent to the Gentiles with promises," or over Isa. 52: "Christ's free redemption"). Nor was this sort of interpretation simply a patristic or Reformation device. It is found in Scripture itself: see 1 Cor. 10:4, where Paul, in speaking of the wilderness experience of the Jews after the Exodus, says that "they drank from the spiritual Rock that followed them, and the Rock was Christ."

The word normally used to describe this "finding of Christ in the Old Testament" is *typology,* or *antityping*—a *type,* or *antitype,* being a prefiguring of a later event. But such a way of defining the concept has a drawback: people take it as positing a merely *mental* connection between, say, Jesus and the Paschal Lamb. Accordingly, what I have been trying to do here (with my analogy to the iceberg and my playing of variations on the theme of sacramentality) is provide a theological basis for seeing this antityping as a *real anticipation,* an *actual pre-presence,* a *prolepsis in fact* of the mystery finally manifested in Jesus. For if we do not posit some such basis, the whole tissue of the Christian view of Scripture as one grand revelation of God in history falls apart. It either degenerates into a series of discrete, incremental bits of weaving, or it unravels into a tangle of arbitrary, imported allegorizations. But with the theological undergirding I have suggested, Scripture's own single-revelation view of itself—not to mention such audacious Christian insistences as the notion that the God of the Old Testament is none other than the Holy and Undivided Trinity—is amply vindicated.

I commend this approach to you, therefore. It saves, quite literally, everything. It leaves all the historical events fully historical, yet it does not limit their sacramentalizing of the mystery to their contemporary significance alone. It allows you to postulate a revelation as progressive as you like, but nonetheless to see its sequential details (even the most primitive of them) as the actions of the one God in the fullness of his mysterious presence. It juxtaposes time and eternity in a way that neither keeps them unsavingly separated nor confounds them in a mishmash that violates both. Principally, though, it does justice to the immediate presence of the entire, eternal mystery to every moment of time and every scrap of space. It lets God be the creating and redeeming God of *all* the particulars of history. It does not confine his action simply to the more notable moments of Scripture, or even to the moments of Scripture alone. It lets you say not only that Jesus died in the Paschal Lamb and in the death of Lazarus, but also that he died in the deaths of six million Jews during the Holocaust—and for that matter in all deaths, everywhere and always. Above all, it allows you to proclaim your faith that in the power of his resurrection, he is present to the whole of creation, not just to those who happen to be Christians. In short, it finally makes solid, earthly sense of Jesus' words, "I, if I be lifted up from the earth, will draw *all* to myself" (John 12:32).

Accordingly, with no apologies for having dragged you through a bit of theological heavy sledding, I go straight to the catena of acted parables—to the remarkable series of tips of the iceberg—that the Gospels present to us at the beginning of Holy Week.

Palm Sunday first (Aland no. 269). The mystery that Jesus is sacramentalizing by riding triumphally into Jerusalem on the back of a donkey is his *parousía,* his coming as a king in peace and as a judge in vindication. Had he been coming as a king to make war, or as a judge to settle scores, he would presumably have come on horseback to signify such aggressive intentions. But even though he made his peaceable disposition clear—even though (as Matthew points out) his choice of a donkey was a fulfillment of the irenic prophecy, "Tell the daughter of Zion: Behold, your king is coming to you, humble, and mounted on an ass" (Matt. 21:5; cf. Zech. 9:9) —the sacramental significance of his action was lost on the crowd that acclaimed him. Expecting only an interventionist, plausible Messiah, they hailed him only as such—only as one who would, then and there and by right-handed power, bring in "the kingdom of our father David that is coming" (Mark 11:10). Nevertheless, as Jesus rides into the city, there is one thing and one thing only uppermost in his mind; namely, his left-handed, implausible death. And he knows in his bones, even if he does not yet realize it in his mind, that this same crowd will paradoxically provide him with the messianic death they refuse even to think about now: on Good Friday, precisely because he will have given them no sustained evidence of right-handed intervention on his part, they will be the very ones who cry, "Crucify him!"

The Triumphal Entry, therefore, is a parable of both grace and judgment. It is a parable of the judgment that descends only on the refusal of grace; and it is a parable of the grace that remains forever sovereign over judgment. For if the peaceable manner of his entry into a city at war with his methods is a judgment on their unwillingness to accept a dying/rising Messiah, so it is also (by being a voluntary going to his death) a proclamation of the grace that will absolve even their nonacceptance of him on the cross: "Father, forgive them" will be his last word on the subject. The iceberg, if you will, will thrust up above the surface of history on Good Friday as well as on Palm Sunday and proclaim for all time the way God perennially works.

The next two tips of the iceberg, however—the next two acted parables in the Holy Week sequence—proclaim grace and judgment not only simultaneously but also in tandem. First comes Jesus' Weeping over Jerusalem (Luke 19:41-44; Aland no. 270), and immediately afterward comes his Cleansing of the Temple (Aland no. 271: the episode is reported at this point by all three synoptics, but much earlier in the Fourth Gospel). In the abstract, it would seem that the Weeping might represent grace, and the Cleansing, judgment; but when the passages are actually examined, that turns out not to be the case. Each event is charged with both; and remarkably, the accounts of the Cleansing of the Temple actually contain more examples of what I have called the vocabulary of grace—more emphasis on littleness, lostness, leastness, etc. as the vehicles of salvation—than does the report of the Weeping over the City. This will become clear as I proceed, so let me begin by dealing with the Weeping first.

As the story opens, Jesus is drawing near to the city (presumably, this episode takes place on Palm Sunday, just prior to his arrival at the gates). Only moments before, Luke reports (Luke 19:39-40), some Pharisees in the crowd say to him, "Master, rebuke your disciples"; and Jesus answers, "I tell you, if these were silent, the very stones would cry out." It would seem, therefore, that even though Jesus has been aware all along that he is riding straight into the teeth of non-acceptance, the fact now hits him emotionally in a peculiarly powerful way. Everything he has predicted is now coming home to roost, and the sad enormity of it overwhelms him with both pity and anger: pity that the city cannot accept him; anger that it will not.

But in the speech that follows, it is anger that gains the upper hand. "If only you could know," he begins graciously enough, "even you, on this day, the things that make for peace. . . ." (I think that the Greek of that half-sentence can actually be read two ways: graciously, as implying "but sadly, you can't"; or judgmentally, as implying "but you damned well won't, as far as I'm concerned"—compare the Greek of Ps. 95:11, quoted in Heb. 3:11.) In any case, the rest of the sentence says, neutrally, that the city just doesn't know these things: "but now they are hid from your eyes." And the remainder of the passage goes on to spell out prophetically the condemning judgment that will be imposed: the city's enemies will surround it, and raze it to the ground together with all its inhabitants, and they will not leave in it one stone upon another *because it did not know the time of its visitation (episkopḗs)*.

The Greek word here for "visitation" is a variant of the word for "bishop" *(epískopos,* overseer) and it provides a springboard for the application of this passage to the whole world as well as to Jerusalem. God's "visitation" of the world—both his mysterious, intimate presence to it below the surface of history and his *parousía* above that surface in the mighty acts of salvation—is the visitation of an overseer, not an avenger. It is the presence of the Good Shepherd, not the wolf (see 1 Pet. 2:25 for the identification of "shepherd" with *episkopos,* and of both with Jesus). But it is the presence of a Shepherd and Bishop who, given the way the world is, can only be seen by that world as an angry judge. For the world, by its own stubborn choice and its own irreversible pride, is going to hell in a handbasket. That is why its messianic overseer weeps: angry tears, judgmental tears, to be sure; but tears nonetheless. Tears from the same Messiah who earlier said, "Jerusalem, Jerusalem . . . , how often have I wanted to gather your children as a hen gathers her chicks under her wings, and you were not willing" (Luke 13:34).

His divine oversight, of course—his all-reconciling *episkopé* —will triumph in the end: to say it again, grace remains forever sovereign over judgment. The new Jerusalem, the new heavens, and the new earth—the whole redeemed order of the new world — will come down from heaven out of God, adorned as a bride for her husband (Rev. 21:1-2). Every tear will be wiped away. But in the meantime, for as long as the world insists on its own oversight—for as long as we will not abandon our domestic madness and our public folly—judgment will inevitably seem sovereign over grace. Guilt will estrange our faces from forgiveness; we will never, by our own devices, find the things that belong to our peace.

And so Jesus proceeds to the next of his acted parables. Going into the temple (still on Palm Sunday, at least in Matthew and Luke), he drives out all who sold and bought in the temple, overturns the tables of the money changers and the seats of those who sold pigeons, and says to them, "My house shall be called a house of prayer, but you make it a den of robbers." His *episkopé* — his visitation, his gracious shepherding and bishoping of creation—once again asserts itself. Of all the places in the world that should have stood witness to grace and truth, the temple was that place; but the world has infected even it, and there is nothing to be done with such a ship of fools but to pronounce upon it the judgment it deserves.

GOD'S ACTION IN HISTORY

Nevertheless, even after he parabolically acts out that judgment, his visitation remains one of grace: "and the blind and the lame [losers all] came to him in the temple, *and he healed them*" (Matt. 21:14).

"But when the chief priests and the scribes saw the wonderful things he did [I am following Matt. 21:15-17 here], and the children [more losers and little ones] crying out in the temple, 'Hosanna to the Son of David,' they were indignant; and they said to him, 'Do you hear what these are saying?' And Jesus said to them, 'Yes; have you never read: *Out of the mouths of babes and nursing children* [yet more of the last and the least] *you have perfected praise*'? And leaving them, he went out of the city to Bethany and lodged there."

Mark and Luke do not report this rhapsody on losing, but John goes it one better: he links the Cleansing of the Temple with the ultimate saving loss, the death and resurrection of Jesus himself. This is not the place to go into John's possible reasons for placing this episode at the beginning of Jesus' ministry—at John 2:13, after the "sign" of changing water into wine at the wedding at Cana. Suffice it to say that this early placement of the Cleansing not only makes good Johannine sense; John's version of the event also makes the same point that Matthew's does. Watch. The Judean authorities, having witnessed the Cleansing, respond to Jesus by asking (John 2:18), "What sign are you showing us by doing these things?" Jesus answers them, "Destroy this temple and I will raise it up in three days." At first, the authorities mock him, thinking he is referring to the temple he has just wrought havoc in: "This temple took forty-six years to build," they say, "and you're going to raise it up in three days?" But Jesus, John notes, was speaking of "the temple of his body"—and he goes on to note that when Jesus was raised from the dead, "his disciples remembered that he said this, and they believed the Scripture and the word that Jesus had said."

It is the sovereignty of grace over judgment all over again. It is the exaltation of losers who are willing to believe in grace over winners who think they can make it on their own. Judg-

99

ment indeed falls on the world; but since the world is populated entirely by losers (in the end, none of us ever wins here) there is hope for everybody. Grace perennially waits for us to accept our destruction and, in that acceptance, to discover the power of the Resurrection and the Life.

Finally, though, in Matt. 21:18-19 and Mark 11:12-14 (Aland no. 272), there follows the bizarre episode of the Cursing of the Fig Tree (Luke omits it at this point, but includes it earlier—transformed, significantly, into a parable of grace— at Luke 13:6-9). Jesus comes back to Jerusalem the following day, and, seeing a fig tree by the side of the road, he goes to it and finds nothing but leaves (Mark adds the comment, "because it was not the season for figs"). Then Jesus says to the tree, "May no one ever eat fruit from you forever" (*eis ton aiōna,* to the age). According to Matthew, "the fig tree withered at once"; Mark, who puts the Cursing of the Fig Tree likewise on Monday, but before the Cleansing of the Temple, delays the discovery of its having withered until Tuesday. In either case, the upshot is similar: Jesus, after an exceptionally harsh, if not unintelligible, act of judgment on the fig tree's unreadiness for him (and by extension, on both Jerusalem's and the world's unreadiness), goes back to grace again. But because Mark strikes the note of grace even more clearly, let me conclude by following him.

As Jesus and his disciples pass by the next morning, they see that the fig tree has "withered away to its roots" (Mark 11:20-26 and parallels; Aland no. 275). Peter remembers what happened the day before and says, "Master, look! The fig tree you cursed has withered." And Jesus answers him, "Have faith (*pístin*) in God. Truly I say to you, whoever says to this mountain [Jerusalem: Mt. Zion], 'Be taken up and be cast into the sea,' and does not doubt in his heart, but believes (*pisteúę̄*) that what he says will come to pass, it will be done for him."

It is tempting, of course, to take this as a general exhortation to prayer; but I think that is the wrong tack in this context. Jesus has been speaking of the judgment of destruction that will fall on Jerusalem (and the world) because it will not forsake what it thinks it knows in favor of what he wants it to believe. Therefore it is the believing, the faith, that should be emphasized in this passage, not the bizarre results—either of praying that a fig tree be cursed or of praying that Jerusalem go flying into the Mediterranean. Jesus is saying that even in the apparently harsh judgments of destruction that he has just issued, faith—trust in him—will still be able to turn death into resurrection. Grace that saves through faith can prevail anywhere.

I realize that such an interpretation is unusual to the point of being idiosyncratic, but stay with me for a moment. Because what Jesus says next (Mark 11:24-25) makes better sense under the aegis of a faith-reading than under the "pray-hard" banner. "For this reason, I tell you," he continues, (I translate literally here) "all things whatsoever you pray for and ask, believe *(pisteúete)* that you have received, and it will be to (or for) you." I don't want to lean too hard on an admittedly contestable point, but it is at least worth noting that the words *it* or *them* (referring to the things asked for) are not actually in the Greek text. It may even be worth suggesting that the "it" in "it will be to you" need not necessarily refer to those things either: "it" just might be something further back and deeper down in Jesus' mind. With great tentativeness, therefore, I am going to suggest that maybe—only maybe—it is possible to interpret the "things" we are supposed to believe we have received as the mystery of grace working in death and destruction, and to interpret the "it" that will be to us or for us as the mystery of resurrection.

Be that as shaky as it may, the rest of the passage bears it out remarkably well. "And whenever you stand praying," Jesus says, "forgive, if you have anything against anyone, so that your Father also who is in heaven may forgive you your trespasses." If this whole monologue of Jesus' is just a lecture on how to damage strangers' fruit trees on a spiritual whim, or take Jerusalem off the map by prayer, what's the point of dragging in forgiveness of all things? That only drops the discourse back into the out-of-context, grunt-and-groan-when-you-pray mode. Forgiveness becomes just one more impossible thing—one more tough and threatening job—that you have to break your spiritual back over. But if Jesus is indeed talking about the forgiving grace that works through the worst, then forgiveness begins to make more sense here.

For how is it that we so frequently run afoul of the worst in our lives? Oh, admittedly some of it comes from the changes and chances of this mortal life, from the malice of the devil or of man—from *the outside,* in short: from things we never wanted and certainly never invited. But a great deal of it comes from *the inside,* from our actually getting a "yes" to a prayer for something we once wanted so badly we could taste it, but which, when we finally got it, turned out to be mostly a millstone around our necks. The friends we now hate, the husbands or wives we are now estranged from, the children who have put both themselves and us on the psychiatrist's couch—all the dire burdens that now fall on us like judgments—all of them were once earnestly invited. Might it not just be that what Jesus is saying here is that *forgiveness* is the only way life's burdens, invited or not, can be lifted? Might he not be telling us, by these two illustrations of the frankly disastrous consequences of prayer (the fig tree withered, Mt. Zion sunk), that even the self-willed calamities of our lives are not hopeless as long as we believe in the gracious One who forgives—and are willing to pass his forgiveness along to others? Might it not mean simply that the world, despite the catastrophes it has brought on itself by its stupid wish-lists, and despite the judgment that must necessarily be pronounced on such follies, is always—even at its willful worst—just one breath away from total reconciliation, *if only it will forgive?*

I, for one, would like to think this passage means that. But whether it does or not, there is no question in my mind that that is what all these acted parables, all these surfacings of the iceberg, have been about—and that *that* is what Jesus calls us to believe. So thank you and goodnight. Whatever else we may be sure or unsure of, at least we know the one thing that belongs to our peace.

CHAPTER EIGHT

The Eye of the Hurricane

The Question of Jesus' Authority; the Two Sons;
the Wicked Tenants

All the rest of Jesus' spoken parables of judgment occupy a space of not more than four days, if you follow Matthew and Luke—or even as few as three, if you follow Mark. His acted parables of messianic authority (Palm Sunday, the Cleansing of the Temple) have now been accomplished: from here on — in the relatively quiet time before the beginning of the passion on Maundy Thursday evening—there is nothing but talk recorded in the Gospels. Jesus, for his part, tells one judgmental story after another and speaks in apocalyptic discourses; the Judean authorities, for theirs, respond with baited questions, trying their best to catch him in a chargeable offense. This is the eye of the hurricane, the ominous calm that is everyone's last chance to speak before the second onslaught of the redemptive storm.

The first two parables he tells in this interlude are those of the Two Sons and the Wicked Tenants (Aland nos. 277, 278); but since these are both presented in the light of the official hostility to him, I shall preface them by dealing first with Aland no. 276: the Questioning of Jesus' Authority by the establishment figures who are out to destroy him (the Gospel passages are Matt. 21:23-27; Mark 11:27-33; and Luke 20:1-8).

"They came again to Jerusalem," Mark says, placing the episode on Tuesday. "And as he was walking in the temple, the chief priests and the scribes and the elders came to him and they said to him, 'By what authority *(exousía)* are you doing these things, or who gave you authority to do them?'" The recurrence at this point of the word *exousía* is one of the notable symmetries in the synoptic Gospels. At the beginning of Jesus' ministry, it was precisely his teaching "as one who had *exousía,* and not as the scribes" (Mark 1:22) that attracted the crowds to him and led the establishment, even at that early date, to "take counsel against him to kill him" (Mark 3:6). Now, at the end, it is that same *exousía* of his, that same sui generis authority—that underivative, even arrogant style of operating by no one's leave but his own—that returns as the *leitmotiv* of the drama. The seemingly interventionist manifestations of it are the cause of the people's enthusiasm at the Triumphal Entry and in the Temple (Jesus has nerve!); and the ultimately non-interventionist mystery of it is the cause of their forsaking him on Good Friday ("Some nerve! We like our Messiahs unique, but not so unique as to die"). But above all, Jesus' *exousía* is the cause of the urgency with which the ruling class now moves to do him in. Between the fear that Jesus will upset their political balancing act with Rome and the resentment they feel at his attacks upon themselves, they decide that his (to them) pretense of *exousía* has to be stopped forthwith. Hence their question, "By what authority? . . ."

But Jesus' *exousía*—his unique claim to an authority based on *who he is,* not on *what he can prove himself to be*—is not something he can justify to their satisfaction. He is asking them to believe in him; they, at best, are trying to decide whether they can find room for him in their minds. And because Jesus knows there is no way of ending such a standoff, he simply contents himself with parrying their thrusts. In the face of their questions, he continually frustrates them by being what he always was, a fox, a rebel, a bad boy who refuses to answer except with questions of his own. "Tell me," he says. "The baptism of John—was it from heaven or from men?" In an instant, he has put them in a bind. If they say, "From heaven," they know he will ask them, "Why then didn't you believe *(episteúsate)* him?" and if they say, "From men," they will have to answer to the people, "because all held that John was really a prophet" (Mark 11:29-32). Accordingly, they run for the first shabby intellectual cover they can find: "We do not know," they answer him. And Jesus, diving nervily into the same cover, replies, "Neither will I tell you by what *exousía* I do these things."

In its form, this exchange is simply an example of Jesus' facility with the tricks of rabbinical argument; but in its substance, it is far more than that. As far as he is concerned, there are only two central considerations in his ministry, now or ever: his own authority—his *exousía* as who he is—and their trust *(pístis)* or distrust in him personally. He is not in the business of giving them arguments that will prove he has some derivative right to their attention; he is only inviting them to believe. This is the hard stone in the gracious peach of his Good News: salvation is not by works, be they physical, intellectual, moral, or spiritual; it is strictly by faith in him. And therefore it is not just these present, official questioners whom he refuses to answer: Jesus never answers any such questions. He frustrates James and John when they ask for seats on his right and his left (Mark 10:35-45); he replies in riddles to the Judean authorities when they demand to know what sign he is showing by cleansing the temple (John 2:13-17); and even at the end, he refuses to give an answer to the apostles when they inquire whether he will "at this time restore the kingdom to Israel" (Acts 1:6). Furthermore, these frustrating refusals go on and on, not only after the ascension but right up to the present day: Jesus obviously does not answer many questions from you or me. Which is why apologetics—the branch of theology that seeks to argue for the justifiability of God's words and deeds—is always such a questionable enterprise. Jesus just doesn't argue. Even when he involves himself in disputations, the most obvious thing about him is that he is refusing to cooperate with his disputers. He does not reach out to convince us; he simply stands there in all the attracting/repelling fullness of his *exousía* and dares us to believe.

I have spent some time on these notes of authority and

faith because they are crucial points in the interpretation of the two parables we are about to take up. They are, in fact, the very nub of the message of the Two Sons and the Wicked Tenants; I intend, therefore, to resist the temptation to let other interpretations put them in the shade. Take the Two Sons first. As it appears in the Gospel (only at Matt. 21:28-32; Aland no. 277), it is presented as the uninterrupted continuation of the wrangle over Jesus' *exousía* we have just dealt with. Moreover, its clinching, final lines are precisely a reference to the ministry of John the Baptist that Jesus has just alluded to. Accordingly, even on the face of the Gospel account, Jesus is holding steadfastly to the same subject he has been pursuing all along.

"What do you think?" he asks the rulers. "A man had two sons; and he went to the first and said, 'Son, go and work in the vineyard today' [flag up: this parable will carry within it not only the force of the immediately previous discussion but that of the Laborers in the Vineyard as well (Matt. 20:1-16)]. And the first son answered, 'I will not'; but afterward he repented and went. And he went to the second and said the same; and he answered, 'I go, Sir,' but did not go. Which of the two," Jesus then asks, "did the will of his father?"

Time for a break, in order to note two false leads in the interpretation of this parable: it is not primarily about the Gentile/Jew controversy in the early church, and it is not at all about works mattering more than words. The Gentile/Jew reading is a wrong start because, while the influx of Gentile Christians on the basis of faith alone is a possible minor point of exposition, it cannot be the main point unless you take this passage as an ecclesiastical gloss rather than as the words of Jesus himself. But to me, that is both cumbersome and unlikely. Jesus is, after all, talking to Jews here. Accordingly, the most likely reading is that the two sons represent two different responses (faith and unfaith), each of which is a response that Jews have made to both John the Baptist and Jesus. Similarly, the works-versus-words reading is a mistake. Jesus is on the subject of faith in his own *exousía*, not on the subject of legalistic fine slicing by which a no that turns into a yes can be construed as a more meritorious work than a yes that turns out to be a no.

In any case, Jesus continues the parable (Matt. 21:31-32) by speaking only of Jews. "Amen, I say to you, the tax collectors and the harlots go into the kingdom before you. For John came to you in the way of righteousness and you did not believe *(episteúsate)* him, but the tax collectors and the harlots believed him; and even when you saw it, you did not afterward repent and believe him."

This is, of course, a parable of judgment. But I want you to note how it is that Jesus shows the imposition of the judgment here. Let me rephrase his question ("Which of the two did the will of his father?") in the form of a series of questions and answers that may help clarify not only his own reasoning but the reasoning of Scripture as a whole:

Q: On which of these two sons will judgment fall?
A: On the second.

Q: Why?
A: Because he did not do the will of his father.

Q: And what then is the father's will?
A: [I quote from Jesus himself, in John 6:40]: "This is the will of my Father, that every one who sees the Son [Jesus — just standing there, and speaking there, and hanging there on the cross] and believes *(pisteúōn)* in him may have everlasting life, and I will raise him up at the last day."

Do you see? The incidental devices by which the two sons arrived at believing or nonbelieving behavior—at faith or unfaith, at a yes-out-of-a-no or at a no-out-of-a-yes—are not the main point. That point is simply that judgment falls adversely on unfaith alone. And it is underscored by Jesus' insistence that the tax collectors and the harlots will go into the kingdom before the rulers. It is not that those disreputable types will be saved because they straightened up and flew right; it is that they will be saved just because they believed. And it is not that the rulers will run a poor second because they took a nosedive into evil works after a previously respectable flight pattern. Like the Pharisee in the Pharisee and the Publican, they are condemned for not repenting of their unfaith—for their faithless nonacceptance of the grace that works by raising the dead. Therefore even the failure to repent of which Jesus finally accuses the rulers is not a moral matter. As a matter of fact, they had no more moral turpitude to repent of than the Pharisee did. They were good people. And as far as the tax collectors and the harlots were concerned, they, like the publican in the parable, had more strikes against them than any mere reform could cancel: they were bad people—losers, outcasts, social dead ducks.

All of this is convincingly present in the parable of the Two Sons, if you scratch beneath its surface. The "repentance" of the one son cannot possibly have removed the factual outrage of his refusal to work; and the shirking of the other cannot have obliterated the prior goodness of his prompt compliance. The first son's initial no to his father remains the insult it always was, and the second son's yes stands as an irrevocable joy. It is not that either the evils of the first are reformed away or that the goodnesses of the second go into the discard; it is just that the one finally, and in living fact, takes his stand on trust in his father's *exousía* while the other in fact repudiates it.

Accordingly, this parable is indeed charged with all the judgment-on-the-refusal-of-grace overtones that are present in the Laborers in the Vineyard. Just as in that parable the last laborers hired get full pay simply as a result of their trusting the word of the lord of the vineyard, and living out that trust for a single, less-than-meritorious hour, so with the first son here. And just as the laborers who worked all day labored only in hope of reward for their works—and refused to trust the lord when he proclaimed grace, not reward, as his only real interest—so with the second son. As a matter of fact, if you wanted to press the parable, you might even postulate that the second son was fully aware of his father's acceptance of his brother's too-easy repentance after insubordination, and that he decided to teach the freewheeling pair of them (especially his father) a lesson. *He* would puncture the tires of all this freedom in faith by just not showing up to do any of the works he was famous for. They thought they could count on *him*, did they? Well, they'd be sorry.

And if you then expand upon the parable, you get an instant application of it to the life of the church in all ages. For no matter how much we give lip service to the notion of free grace and dying love, *we do not like it*. It is just too . . . indiscriminate. It lets rotten sons and crooked tax farmers and common tarts into the kingdom, and it thumbs its nose at really good people. And it does that, gallingly, for no more reason than the Gospel's shabby exaltation of dumb trust over worthy works. Such nonsense, we mutter in our hearts; such heartless, immoral folly. We'll teach God, we say. We will continue to sing "Amazing Grace" in church; but we will jolly well be judicious when it comes to explaining to the riffraff what it actually means. We will assure them, of course, that God loves them and forgives them, but we will make it clear that *we* expect them to clean up their act before we clasp them seriously to our bosom. We do not want whores and chiselers and practicing gays (even if they *are* suffering with AIDS) thinking they can just barge in here and fraternize. Above all, we do not want drunk priests, or ministers who cheat on their wives with church organists, standing up there in the pulpit telling us that God forgives such effrontery. *We* never did such things. Why, we can hardly even bear to think. . . .

Do you see now? We are second sons, elder brothers, respectable Pharisees, twelve-hour, all-day laborers whose moral efforts have been trampled on by the Feet Beautiful upon the Mountains. We are resentful at being the butts of the divine joke of grace that says nothing matters except plain, old, de facto, yes-Jesus faith. And when we institutionalize that resentment by giving the impression that the church is not for sinners and gainsayers, we are a disgrace to the Gospel—a bushel of works hiding the Light of the world. We are under judgment. Oh, yes; we say we believe. But what we believe is largely an ethico-theological construct of our own devising, a system in our heads that will make the world safe for democracy, and for thrifty, brave, clean, and reverent ex-sinners like ourselves. Like the second son, our only real trust is in our own devices. Just trusting Jesus—the friend of tax collectors and sinners, the one who, while we are still sinners, dies for the ungodly—is not our idea of how to run a lifeline.

"Diffidam mihi, fidam in te," said Augustine to God; "I will distrust myself, I will trust in you." The first son had the grace to distrust his own first formulation of what was actually going on between him and his father and to eat crow, turning his self-regarding no of works into an other-regarding yes of faith. And for that faith, he is commended as having done the will of his father—the whole will, not just some preliminary velleity on his father's part but *all he ever wanted*. And that will is one thing and one only: believing. It is trust in him—anytime, anywhere, anyhow. But the second son turned Augustine's prayer around: *"Fidam in meipsum, diffidam tibi"*: "I will trust myself, I will distrust you." He kept scores where his father kept none, books where his father had stopped making entries; and for that reliance on works (nasty, negative, I'll-teach-them works), he is condemned.

So it is with me, if I am honest. And so it is with you. The Father's will for you—his whole will, his entire plan of salvation—is that you believe in Jesus, nothing more. He has already forgiven you, he has already reconciled you, he has already raised you up together with Jesus and made you sit together in heavenly places with him. And better yet, Jesus himself has already pronounced upon you the approving judgment of having done his Father's will. But if you do not believe him—if you insist on walking up to the bar of judgment on your own faithless feet and arguing a case he has already dismissed—well, you will never hear the blessed silence of his uncondemnation over the infernal racket of your own voice. "He who argues his own case has a fool for a lawyer" is true in any court. But in this court you will be more than a fool if you try that trick. You will be an idiot. There is no case. There is no evidence against you. And there is no courtroom to display your talents in. It is all quashed, all over but the fun of having an eternal drink with the Judge who makes Harry Stone look serious. This is the Gospel as *Night Court*. All you have to do is hoist your glass and say, "Yes, Judge. Cheers! *Skal! Salute! Ein Prosit!* Bottoms up!" The whole thing, you see, stands forever on its head: the last shall be first—just for believing.

The parable that immediately follows the Two Sons takes up the same topics of faith and *exousía* from an opposite point of view. The story of the Wicked Tenants looks at the picture of rejection-by-unbelief from God's side rather than from ours. It occurs in all three synoptics (at Matt. 21:33-46; Mark 12:1-12; and Luke 20:9-19; Aland no. 278); but I shall continue to follow Matthew's account for two reasons. First, because it forms a logical sequel to the parable of the Two Sons, which only Matthew records. But second, because it is the fuller version. Indeed, if you will permit me an aside on the subject of biblical criticism, its very fullness serves as an argument in favor of the ancient view of the relationships among the synoptic Gospels. The modern view, of course, is that Mark was written first and that his Gospel was thus available to both Matthew and Luke; it also holds that, along with their own peculiar sources, designated as M and L, they had had material from a source common to them both but missing from Mark—a source designated as Q. In earlier times, however, it was generally assumed that Matthew came first, that Mark subsequently revised and abridged Matthew, and that Luke then used both of them, adding his own material where he thought appropriate. For well over a hundred years now, the modern view has reigned unquestioned and the ancient one has been treated as having no respectable claims at all. But if you look carefully at the parable of the Wicked Tenants in all three Gospels, you will see that the matter is not quite so clear-cut.

For one thing, Matthew and Mark agree at certain points and Luke is the odd man out (compare the first verse of the parable in all three accounts). Score one for the old, "updated abridgment" theory of Mark. The ancients were not just blindly caving in to the tradition that put Matthew first in the canon of Scripture; there are a number of instances in the synoptic Gospels where Luke inexplicably omits certain Markan passages which, on the modern view, he supposedly had right in front of him. See, for example, the parable of the Mustard Seed (Aland no. 209; Mark 4:30-32 and parallels), the passage on Divorce and Celibacy (Aland no. 252; Mark 10:2-12 and parallels), or the passage on the Sons of Zebedee and their request to sit on Jesus' right and left in glory (Aland no. 263; Mark 10:35-45 and parallels). But for another thing, Mark and Luke sometimes agree against Matthew (compare, in this parable, Mark 12:4-5 and parallels), suggesting that when Luke did use Mark, he did so because he felt it was a better account than Matthew's — provided, of course, he had access to the Matthean version.

My purpose in mentioning all this is not to advocate the abandonment of the modern view (on balance, it does seem to explain the complexities of the synoptic interrelationships a bit better). I only want to note that those interrelationships are indeed complex, and that it may well be true that no hypothesis about them will ever cover the ground with complete satisfaction. In any case, back to the text in Matthew.

"Hear another parable," Jesus says, picking up right after the story of the Two Sons. "There was a householder who planted a vineyard, and set a hedge around it, and dug a winepress in it, and built a tower, and let it out to tenants, and went into another country." Once again, Jesus recurs to the image of the vineyard, echoing not only his own parables, but also such passages as Isa. 5:7, "The vineyard of the Lord of hosts is the house of Israel, and the people of Judah are his pleasant planting." As in the parable of the Two Sons, I am once again going to resist the temptation to leap to a Jew/Gentile interpretation here. Jesus is still talking to Jews at this point: while such an interpretation is fair enough for certain expository purposes (and is even supported by the uniquely Matthean passage in verse 43), the main thrust of the parable goes to the more general matter of rejection of Jesus' *exousía* by unfaith.

(Verse 43's consequent giving of the kingdom to another "nation [*éthnei*] producing the fruits" of faith is simply a forceful, prophetic instance of the perils of that rejection.)

Israel, the parable is saying, has been chosen by God as his vineyard and God has let that vineyard out to the tenants now in charge, namely, the Judean authorities whose hostility and defective stewardship Jesus is now addressing. Look at the text: "When the season (*kairós*, high time, due season) of fruit drew near, he [the householder] sent his servants to get his fruit." Plainly, in adducing this first group of servants, Jesus is referring to the prophets who, as he sees it, have prepared the way for his own coming—and who, in their own time, were no more acceptable to the authorities than Jesus is now. As he puts it, the tenants took those servants and "beat one, killed another, and stoned another." But then, after having the householder send still more servants to the same fate, Jesus has him decide to send his son to them, saying, "They will respect my son." Just as plainly, this is a setup for the condemnation of the authorities of Jesus' day.

In strict logic, the parable becomes tortured, if not fantastic at this point: Jesus is clearly trying to show their rejection as folly. There is no good reason, for example, why the tenants should alter their unfaithful stewardship now (the son is just one more interference with their plans); correspondingly, there is also no good reason, in real life, for Jesus to hope that the authorities he is dealing with will alter their unbelief (to them, he is simply a dangerous nuisance). Furthermore, the reason the tenants give for their plan to kill the householder's son is equally absurd: there is no real chance that murdering the heir of the vineyard will result in their inheriting it, especially since the householder is still alive, well, and breathing down their necks at the end of the parable (see Matt. 21:40). The only way their reasoning could make sense is if they assumed that the householder was so far away (or, in the case of the Judean authorities, that the day of reckoning was so far off) that they could live out the time of their stewardship before the judgment descended upon them.

That, of course, is a possible interpretation: and if you like it, it enables you to open up the parable considerably. Watch. The precise assumption of the authorities facing Jesus is that the judgment is a long way in the future. Their further assumption is that when it does come, it will not only be recognizable as a right-handed, score-evening operation that will make Israel the top dog of the world; it will also feature a Messiah (or a Son of man) who will himself be recognizable as a nose-punching interventionist. They are not at all prepared for the appearance of some ineffective messianic pretender whose idea of saving action is aggravating God's representatives into exterminating him—which, of course, is exactly what Jesus' paradoxical arrival on their scene looks like to them. And because they will not trust him in such a mild arrival, because they can conceive only of their own, vindictive version of the coming in judgment, for that very reason, the real, vindicating judgment—the judgment that will inquire only if they have trusted, not how well or badly they managed—will fall on them anyway, condemning their unfaith.

Therefore, having postulated the fantastic, pointless killing of the householder's son, Jesus asks the clinching, rhetorical question: "When the owner (*kýrios*, lord) of the vineyard comes, what will he do to those tenants?" And they answer him ("they," presumably, being the authorities Jesus is aiming this parable at): "He will put those wretches to a miserable death and let out the vineyard to other tenants who will give him the fruits in their seasons *(kairoís)*." The setup, you see, has worked perfectly. Jesus has gotten them to say exactly what he would have said himself: the stewardship of the mystery of salvation will be taken away from the present authorities who have exercised it in unfaith and it will be given to others who will exercise it in faith. Moreover, those others will be able to stand at the judgment that looks only at faith because they will have done the "one thing necessary": they will have accepted, rather than rejected, the Son in his paradoxically mild coming. They will have recognized his all-reconciling, left-handed *exousía* and they will stand approved because of their trust. But the authorities—even though they, too, are in fact just as much *within* the power of his reconciliation—will have cut themselves off from that power.

Jesus then goes on to tie up the parable (Matt. 21:42-46). He says to them, "Have you never read the Scriptures [he is continuing to drive home the point that the Old Testament—to which he has referred by his allusions to the vineyard and to the prophets—promises *his* kind of Messiah, not theirs]: 'The stone that the builders rejected has become the very cornerstone; this was the Lord's doing, and it is marvelous (*thaumasté,* astonishing, even shocking) in our eyes'? [he is quoting from Ps. 118:22-23]." Jesus is saying quite clearly, in other words, that not only is his own mild *exousía* unacceptable to their unfaith; it is also and nevertheless—*in its very unacceptability*—the cornerstone of their salvation, even though they will not trust it. The world is saved only by his passion, death, and resurrection, not by any of the devices that, in its unbelief, it thinks it can take refuge in. Furthermore, that same unacceptability will be the cornerstone of their judgment and of the world's—a truth that Matthew will set forth as Jesus' final word before the passion in the parable of the Last Judgment (Matt. 25:31-46). In that great scene, where the sheep are finally separated from the goats, the criterion for the rewarding of the sheep is nothing other than their blind acceptance by faith of a king who has appeared to the world only under the guise of the last, the lost, the least, and the little. Even the righteous, you see, will know of no *reason* for their vindication; they will only have *experienced* it through the King's paradoxical presence on the underside of creation. They will simply have trusted; and that trust will have already brought them home justified. And as for the goats . . . well, the wicked, too, will have experienced the same presence (the authorities of Jesus' day, for example, were as *involved* in his redeeming death as anybody—Caiaphas, the Sanhedrin, even Judas, were all intimate with his saving *exousía*); but they will not have trusted. They will have been justified and they will have been brought home; but because of the blindness of their unbelief, they will have cut themselves off from the salvation they already had—from the favorable judgment that, but for the noise of their own works, they would otherwise have heard.

Finally, though, Jesus prophetically spells out the end result of the authorities' faithless stewardship of the mystery. "Therefore I tell you, the kingdom of God will be taken away from you and given to a nation producing the fruits of it." Then, referring back to himself as the cornerstone, he says, "And he who falls on this stone will be broken to pieces; but when it falls on anyone it will crush him to dust." This last verse, while less well supported by the textual evidence, still makes perfectly good sense as the concluding line of the parable. It is the generalizing of the judgment that Jesus made specific in the verse before. His paradoxical messiahship is a great stone in the whole world's way: Christ Jesus, as Paul said later in 1 Cor. 1:23, is a stumbling block *(skándalon)* to the Jews, and foolishness *(mōrían)* to the Greeks. The world perennially trips over him in unbelief; and when he comes in judgment to its unfaith, his vindication of it by grace through faith simply grinds to powder the irrelevant, lost life on which it chose to rely.

The authorities, predictably, respond to this statement by trying once again to arrest Jesus. But fearing the multitudes—prudently apprehensive that a popular uproar might bring down the political house of cards that has been their life's work—they put off their plans till they can con the populace into being ground to a powder along with them. Mark and Luke add the detail here that "they perceived that he had told this parable against them" — a perception that any five-year-old could have come up with, but that still deserves a final word. For Jesus *was* against them. And he is against the world, too. He stands in judgment against everyone who will not accept his acceptance of the world by faith alone; but he brings down his gavel only on the folly that will not see that *he judges nothing else*—not goodness, not badness, not anything. And that is such a strange kind of againstness, such a blessed resistance of the world's insistence on judgment by works, that you'd think it would make us all laugh out loud. But the self-justifying world (including an alarmingly large number of Christians who think that being well behaved is more important to God than just trusting his forgiveness) can see it—and him—only as a threat. As any preacher who seriously preaches the Gospel of grace can tell you, the troops are not amused by the prospect of absolutely free salvation. The first instinct of most Christians, after they have smiled indulgently at the preacher's charmingly easygoing concept of salvation, is to nail him to the wall for knocking the props out from under divine retribution for nasty deeds. They do not want grace, they want law. Like the stupid tenants in the parable, they try to stop the coming of the paradoxical Power that alone can keep them in business, and they take their refuge in a lot of prudential nonsense that only insures their going out of it.

They don't stop the Power, of course. Jesus died for the sins of those who killed him—even for the sins of unbelief by which *we* kill him all over again. In the end, though, it is just sad. How unhappy to put ourselves on the losing end of a deal that even our messing up can't really sour! How melancholy not to believe that all he ever wanted was for us to believe!

How just plain dumb!

CHAPTER NINE

The Deluge of Judgment by Mercy

The King's Son's Wedding

The parable of the King's Son's Wedding (Matt. 22:1-14; Aland no. 279) is quite plainly a variation on the parable of the Great Banquet in Luke 14:15-24. But when the two versions are compared, their differences of tone, content, and context are so marked as to make you wonder whether they even deserve the name parallel passages. You pay your money and take your choice, of course, as to how they got that different. For example, some critics like to assign responsibility for the Matthean version to some first- or second-century ecclesiastical source. But my dollar goes down on a more economical explanation, namely, that the parable appears twice because Jesus told it twice. Like a good preacher, however, he did not simply reach into the barrel and use previous sermons unchanged; he varied his material, giving even an old parable a new form for a new occasion.

Take the present parable as an instance. Jesus told it in its first form (in Luke) at a meal in the house of one of the chief Pharisees: in that context, it was predominantly a parable of grace, with a short judgmental kicker at the end. On second telling, however (in Matthew, during Holy Week), he transformed it into a full-fledged parable of judgment, with grace tucked down below as the subtext. I leave it to you to compare the two in detail; for myself—since I have already treated Luke's version in the previous volume, *The Parables of Grace*—

118

I proceed directly to the Matthean rendering, reminding you only of my insistence that, even when he speaks in judgment, Jesus is careful to make grace sovereign over all.

The story occurs in Matthew with the simplest of introductions: "And again Jesus spoke to them in parables, saying. . . ." The logical antecedent of the "them" is of course the chief priests and Pharisees (Matt. 21:45-46) against whom Jesus has just spoken (and acted out) his immediately preceding parables of judgment—and who, in fact, are trying to arrest him and kill him. We should expect, therefore, that this version will be far "hotter," far more filled with severity and even death, than his previous telling of the story over dessert and coffee at a dinner party; and so it is. But before we dwell on its uniqueness, I want you to put in the back of your mind two striking details that Jesus carries over from the earlier version. First, he uses the imagery of a wedding (*gámos*) in both presentations of the parable: in Matthew, the word occurs in the opening words of the parable itself; in Luke, it occurs in the immediately preceding parable (14:7-8) shortly before he relates the parable of the Great Banquet. Accordingly, since I have been insisting all through this book on a full-court, whole-New-Testament press in my interpretation of the parables, I want you to set this parable not only in the context of the Gospels but also in the light of the wedding that is the climactic image of Scripture, the final wrap-up of the entire Bible, namely, the Marriage Supper (*deípnon*) of the Lamb (Rev. 19:9ff.).

The second detail follows logically from that: in both versions, Jesus makes extensive use of the imagery of a festive meal. In Luke, he not only tells the parable while he is "eating bread on the sabbath" in the Pharisee's house; he also uses the word *dochē* (banquet, reception, Luke 14:13) just before he tells the story and the word *deípnon* (supper, banquet, Luke 14:16, 17, 24) in the parable itself. And in Matthew, he uses the word *áriston* (breakfast, noonday dinner, feast, Matt. 22:4) to specify the nature of the party the king gives to celebrate his son's wedding. Add therefore to your computer memory bank as many dinner parties, suppers, and wedding receptions as you can gather up out of Scripture: not only the final Supper of the Lamb (Rev. 19), but the marriage feast at Cana of Galilee (John 2), the Last Supper (Matt. 26; Mark 14; Luke 22), the evening meal at Emmaus on the night of Easter Day (Luke 24), the breakfast of broiled fish by the lakeside at one of Jesus' resurrection appearances (John 21)—and for good measure, the Passover meal in Exod. 12, all sabbath meals everywhere, the feast for the prodigal son (Luke 15), and the Lord's Supper throughout Christian history. In other words, this parable must be read in the context of all the gracious invitations to "sit together in Christ Jesus" (Eph. 2:6), be they Old Testament antitypes, Gospel events, present realities, or eschatological promises. The world has been summoned precisely to a party—to a reconciled and reconciling dinner *chez* the Lamb of God; judgment is pronounced only in the light of the acceptance or declination of that invitation.

For that reason, I simply note the immediate context of the parable and move on: Jesus is speaking for openers here about the rejection by the authorities of his invitation to believe in him. But only for openers. The reach of this parable goes far beyond the Jews of Jesus' own time, and even beyond the Jew/Gentile conflict in the early church: it ultimately defines the nature both of the salvation he offers to the whole world and of the judgment he pronounces on the rejection of that offer. It is, in a word, catholic; I will not sell it short by dwelling on parochial interpretations.

"The kingdom of heaven," Jesus begins (tying the story back to all the parables of a mysterious, actual, catholic kingdom he told earlier in his ministry), "may be compared to a king who gave a marriage feast *(gámous)* for his son." Score a happy point for the all-reconciling party and its preeminence as a biblical image. God, the King, is not mad at anybody: because of his Son—because his Son, by death and resurrection, has drawn all creation to himself as the bride of the Lamb—God wills above all to celebrate. And because when God is happy, everybody should be happy, he extends a gracious invitation to join him in his joy: "And he sent his servants to call those who were invited to the marriage feast." Sadly, though, the situation is not that simple: those who were invited, Jesus says, "would not come." Score a sad point, therefore, for the unhappy truth that the world is full of fools who won't believe a good thing when they hear it. Free grace, dying love, and unqualified acceptance might as well be a fifteen-foot crocodile, the way we respond to it: all our protestations to the contrary, we will sooner accept a God we will be fed to than one we will be fed by.

But since Jesus, in telling the parable, now goes on a roll, let us roll with him in the interpretation. The king, undaunted, sends yet more servants: "Tell those who are invited," he commands them, "Behold, I have made ready my feast *(áriston)*, my oxen and my fat calves are killed, and everything is ready; come to the marriage feast." The invited guests, however, make light of it (the Greek is *amelésantes:* disregard, reject, care nothing for, not give a damn about), and they go off, one to his farm and another to his business interests — while the rest make crystal clear to the king what they really think of his monomaniacal insistence on having a party: they seize his servants; they treat them disgracefully; and last but not least, they kill them.

It seems an odd way to run a social life. Most of us are content with just thinking such thoughts: "Another one of those ghastly slow leaks the Hopkinsons try to pass off as a blowout? Why don't we tell them the mailman stepped on a land mine in the lawn and we never got the invitation?" But Jesus is out to stigmatize the incongruous enormity of the rejection, so he insists on nothing less than heaps of murdered mailmen. And he follows it with an absolute festival of death presided over by the king himself. Carrying the note of deadly seriousness to its logical extreme — driving home the nail of an unappeasable determination to celebrate, and not caring that he leaves brutal hammer marks all over the woodwork of his story — he has the king respond in kind to the depredations of the first-invited guests: "The king was angry," Jesus says, "and he sent his soldiers and destroyed those murderers and burned their city." The scene is straight out of the *A-Team:* bazookas firing, napalm enveloping ladies in summer frocks, Rolls Royces being blown up by TOW missiles, hundred-room mansions being burned to the ground. But unlike TV, it features real blood and genuine corpses. This is not just the old Newport-Southampton social snub; this is crossing people off your list for good.

Please note, though, the real reason for such ferocity. Who in fact were all these corpses lying around like so much cord-wood? They were the people who had a right to be at a royal wedding. They were the nobility, the jet set, the stars of stage, screen, and TV. They were, in short, the beautiful and the good. They did not lack for socially acceptable good works: they had the Mercedes Benzes, the Dior gowns, and the sixty-five-foot yachts; above all, they had the *style* to make even a royal wedding look better. But for all that, they were totally lacking in the trust, the faith, that is the only divinely acceptable quality. And so they take their place in Jesus' cavalcade of winners who lose: they are the Pharisee in the temple reading off his list of good deeds; they are Zacchaeus with his speech about what an honest crook he is; and they are you, and they are me. They are all of us who live in the twin certainties that our good works will earn us the right to attend the Supper of the Lamb, and that God's good nature will absolve us from having to sit through it if we happen to have other plans. Why the ferocity, then? Simply this: since neither they nor we could possibly be wronger about either of those two certainties, Jesus insists on displaying both of them as dead wrong. Salvation is not by works, and the heavenly banquet is not an option. We are saved only by our acceptance of a party already in progress, and God has paid for that party at the price of his own death. And since he counts only those two things—only faith and grace—nothing else counts. Outside of the party, there is no life at all.

Which is why Jesus now has the king proceed to what for him is plan B, but what for God has been plan A all along: "Then he said to his servants, 'The wedding is ready, but those invited were not worthy' [in their reliance on their own worth, they lost completely the sole worthiness of faith]; go therefore into the streets of the city and invite to the marriage feast as many as you find.' And those servants went out into the streets and gathered all whom they found, *both bad and good.*"

Stop right there. This last detail is not just a peculiarity of this parable; it is practically the hallmark of Jesus' major parables of the kingdom and of grace. In the Sower, a catholic sowing has both good and evil results, all of which are within the kingdom. In the Wheat and the Weeds, good and evil are allowed to grow together until the harvest. In the Net, the kingdom gathers of every kind. And in the Good Samaritan, the Prodigal Son, and the Pharisee and the Publican, Jesus goes out of his way to make heroes of life's losers. Evil, in short, is not a problem for the kingdom: it has already been aced out by the power of Jesus' death and resurrection. The only thing that can possibly be a problem for the kingdom is a faithless nonacceptance of God's having solved the problem of evil all by himself, and without ever once having mentioned the subject of reform. He does not invite the good and snub the bad. He invites us all, while we are yet sinners; and he simply asks us to trust that invitation. And therefore because the remaining inhabitants of his kingdom, good and bad, did just that—because the working poor and the walking wounded, the bag ladies, the prostitutes, and the derelicts drinking Muscatel in doorways just said yes and came to the wedding—they are all home free at the party: "the wedding hall," Jesus says, "was filled with guests."

It is necessary here, I think, to supply a detail in the parable—a detail made reasonable by the events that are shortly to unfold. Since the types who have now been dragooned into the festivities right off the streets could not possibly have had tuxedos and ball gowns in their shopping carts and brown paper bags, I am going to postulate that the king, in order to give the royal wedding a properly royal ambience, supplied his last-minute guests with suitable clothes on the way in. He opened the royal wardrobe and had his gentlemen and ladies in waiting carry its entire contents down to the front door of the palace. Then, as each one approached, he or she was given something splendid to wear: a Bill Blass original, a Balenciaga creation, whatever.

Now then. The king, satisfied that he has done everything needed to make this the party to end all parties, comes in to survey the splendor of the scene. And what does he see? He sees a perfect spectacular gathering, inexplicably marred by one character totally out of character. Make this man's clothes any style you like: shabby genteel, seedy tweedy, skidrow disreputable or punk-rock garish—all they have to be is inappropriate enough to make him a sore thumb in the royal eye. So the king goes over to him and addresses him with a word that is by now familiar to you as a less-than-friendly greeting: "Buster *(hetaíre),*" he says, "how did you get in here without a wedding garment?" And the gentleman in question, Jesus tells us, "was speechless."

I want you to strike a trial balance on the entries in the parable so far. Entry one: the first-invited guests were all recipients of the king's favor. By his gracious invitation to the wedding, he had said to every last one of them, "You're okay in my book; I want you at my party." The *invitation,* you see, is the principal judgment in this parable—the sentence of vindication from which all the incidental judgments in the story subsequently proceed. It is a judgment filled with grace, and it never once, through the whole parable, loses its status as such. But when it is refused in distrust—when the first guests on the list contradict the king's "You're okay" with their own overwrought refusal to believe him—it simply descends on them. But it does not lose its vindicating character: he still wills nothing but the party. If they will not accept his vindication, that is no skin off his nose: he will rub them, still vindicated, off his list of fun people and go hunt for others who can recognize a good deal when they hear it.

Entry two: the guests invited as replacements are likewise recipients of the king's favor. He doesn't care a fig that they look like pigs and smell worse. He doesn't care that they don't know *hors d'oeuvres* from Havana cigars. He doesn't care that they eat with their hands and blow their noses without handkerchiefs. In other words, he does not make any stipulations about them at all. They do not have to get their act together in order to be worthy of the party, any more than the prodigal son had to guarantee amendment of life before getting the fatted calf. They have only, like the prodigal, to accept the acceptance and go with the flow. The king and the father, you see, are party people. They will take only yes for an answer; anybody who wants to say no has gone to hell already.

Entry three: all of the above is as true of the man without the wedding garment as it was of all the rest. Nobody in the parable is outside the king's favor; everybody starts out by being, as far as the king himself is concerned, irrevocably *in*. The invitation that is the judgment stands forever, reaching out to all.

Trial balance, therefore: *Nobody is kicked out who wasn't already in.* Hell may be an option; but if it is, it is one that is given us only after we have already received the entirely non-optional gift of sitting together in the heavenly places in Christ Jesus. And even for those in hell, God never withdraws that gift because, as Paul says in Rom. 11:29: "The gifts and the calling of God are without repentance *(ametaméleta)*." Please note the Greek in that quotation, because it proves the sum we have just arrived at for all these entries. The root *mel* (meaning "care") in *ametaméleta* is the same root that appears in the word *amelēsantes,* used to describe the disdain of the first-invited guests at Matt. 22:5. (*Amelēsantes* is formed from *a,* "not," plus *mel,* "care"; *ametaméleta* is formed from *a,* "not," plus *metá,* "change," plus *mel,* "care.") Put that all together and you get the picture: we, like the guests, may cease to care about our acceptance, but God never has a change of heart about having offered us acceptance in the first place. Accordingly, while this parable certainly says that God, like the king, will tell those who refuse to trust him to go to hell, hell nevertheless remains radically unnecessary: there will never be any *reasons,* from God's point of view, for anyone to end up there, precisely because God in Jesus has made his grace, and not our track record, the sole basis of salvation. There is therefore now no condemnation to the world as it is held in

Christ Jesus, because there is nothing in the world, neither height, nor depth, nor any other thing—and especially not our long-since-cancelled sins—that can separate us from the love of God that is in Christ Jesus our Lord. The entire world is home free at the eternal party. The only ones who will not enjoy the Marriage Supper of the Lamb are those who, in the very thick of its festivities, refuse to believe they are at it.

On then with the rest of the parable. The man without the wedding garment is speechless precisely because there are no good reasons that unfaith can give for not trusting such a sweet deal. But bad reasons? Alas, there are plenty. Try a few on him for size:

1. (assuming he was one of the first-invited guests and that he just happened to be out of town when the king's SWAT team paid their call): "If he thinks I'm going to put on an un-fitted tuxedo and hobnob with all those deadbeats. . . ."

2. (assuming he was dragged to the party with group two): "Hey! I want to be recognized for myself, not just accepted because somebody put a monkey suit on me."

3. (assuming he was a gate-crasher): "Maybe if I say nothing and just look dumb, he won't notice how poorly I'm dressed."

Do you see? If he had said anything, anything at all—if he had, even for the worst and most stupid of reasons, *put himself in relationship with the king*—he would have been alright. There is nothing to which a king who operates for no reasons whatsoever cannot give an absolving reply:

to #1   "Oh, just shut up, will you, and have a drink on the house."

to #2   "Dummy! The monkey suits are just for fun; it's the people in them I went to the bother of dragging here. Try the caviar; it's real Beluga."

to #3   "Turkey! You actually think I invited all these losers because they passed some kind of test? Relax; this whole party is *free*."

But because the man said nothing—because he would not

bring himself to relate to the king in any way—all the reassurances the king might have given him remain unheard. And so Jesus brings down on him the sentence of condemnation that he has already invoked upon himself by not trusting: "Bind him hand and foot," he has the king say to the servants, "and throw him into the outer darkness—out there where there is only weeping and gnashing of teeth. For many are called (*klētoí*) but few are chosen (*eklektoí*)."

Jesus is not always this harsh. In the parable of the Prodigal Son, where he is at pains to portray unqualified grace and acceptance, he has the father go out and plead with the elder brother, reassuring him of their unbreakable relationship. But then that may be because the elder brother was willing to bellyache openly about the indiscriminateness of grace. He made a godawful speech, but at least he wasn't speechless: grace still looks to triumph in the end. In this parable, though (as in the parable of the Coins), it is judgment that finally has the last word—judgment that falls like a thunderclap on the refusal of grace, and that, in the process, defines the true nature of hell. For hell, ultimately, is not the place of punishment for sinners; sinners are not punished at all; they go straight to heaven just for saying yes to grace. Hell is simply the nowhere that is the only thing left for those who will not accept their acceptance by grace—who will not believe that at three o'clock on a Friday afternoon, free for nothing, the Lamb slain from the foundation of the world actually declared he never intended to count sins in the first place.

What then do I make of, "Many are called but few are chosen"? Just this. The sad truth of our fallen condition is that we don't want anything to do with a system of salvation that works by grace through faith. We want our merits, sleazy though they may be, rewarded—and we want everybody else's obviously raunchy behavior punished. We are like pitiful little bargain-hunters going to a used-car lot with $265 worth of hard-earned cash in our pockets and looking for the ultimate transport of delight. But just as we are about to give up and go away, the salesman comes up to us with a smile on his face.

"You really want a car?" he whispers in our ear. "Come around to the back of the lot. Have I got a deal for you!" And back there, gleaming in the sun, is a brand-new Porsche. "It's yours for free," he says. "The boss just likes you; here are the keys."

Many are called: there is no one in the whole world, good, bad, or indifferent, who isn't walked around to the back of the lot by the divine Salesman and offered heaven for nothing. But few are chosen: because you know what most of us do? First thing—before we so much as let ourselves sink into the leather upholstery or listen to the engine purr—we get suspicious. We walk around the car and kick the tires. We slam the doors. We jump up and own on the bumpers to test the shocks. And then, even if we do decide to take it, we start right in worrying about the warranty, fussing about the cost of insuring a sports car, and even—God help us—fuming about whether, if our no-good neighbor came in here, *he* might be offered a Rolls Royce Silver Cloud. But God doesn't help us—at least not with all that tough-customer routine. He just sits up there in the front office and remains Mr. Giveaway, the Mad Dog Tyson of Parousia Motors, the Crazy Eddy of Eternity whose prices are *insane*. He gives heaven to absolutely everybody: nothing down, no interest, no payments. And he makes hell absolutely unnecessary for anybody. The only catch is, you have to be as crazy as God to take the deal, because your every instinct will be to distrust such a cockamamy arrangement. You have to be willing to believe in an operation that would put any respectable God out of the deity business.

Which, nicely enough, lands us right back at the parable: a king who throws parties any other king would be ashamed of, representing a God who refuses to act like one; and a hell only for idiots who insist on being serious.

CHAPTER TEN

The Waters of Judgment Rise

The Authorities Challenge Jesus; the Synoptic Apocalypse

The next parables to appear in the Gospels—the Fig Tree, the Flood, and the Faithful Servant/Bad Servant (Aland nos. 293, 296, and 297)—all occur at the end of Matt. 24. But since they function there as the finale of a long section of nonparabolic material (Aland nos. 280-292; Matt. 22:15–24:31 and parallels), and since the synoptic writers report this section as Jesus' words during Holy Week, I am going to devote an entire chapter to it before turning to the parables themselves. I think it important to do this because the section constitutes essential stage-setting not only for the parables in question but also for the passion narrative itself. Bear with me, then. My aim will not be to comment in detail on the several passages but rather to give just so much of their gist as will enable you to follow the thread of Jesus' thinking through them all.

The material at hand falls into two parts. The first (Aland nos. 280-286) contains a series of exchanges between Jesus and various Jerusalem authorities, culminating in Jesus' Lament over Jerusalem and his observations about the Widow's Mite. In it, we see him constantly fencing with the scribes, Pharisees, Herodians, and Sadducees, all the while building up a judgmental head of steam that will explode in the immediately following passages. The second part is the explosion itself (Aland nos. 287-297)—a discourse commonly referred to as the synoptic apocalypse because of its style and eschatological content. In this section, Jesus speaks prophetically and warningly of the end *(télos)*, and he proclaims the signs of his *parousía* (presence, coming) that will mark that end.

First section first. Immediately after the parable of the King's Son's Wedding, Matthew reports (Matt. 22:15; Aland no. 280), the Pharisees go and take counsel how to ensnare Jesus with questions. As a result, they send their disciples and some of Herod's party to him with a prepared script: after a bit of unctuous flattery about his reputation for truth telling and his independence of mind, these flunkies are supposed to get him to answer a catch question. The object of the game is to set him up so that if he answers one way the Roman authorities will see him as seditious, and if he answers in another, the Jewish authorities will brand him a blasphemer. And so they do. "Tell us," they challenge him, "is it lawful [for Jews, that is] to pay taxes to Caesar, or not?" But Jesus, aware of their subterfuge (Matthew calls it "malice," Mark, "hypocrisy," and Luke, "craftiness"), falls back once again on the rabbinical trick of answering a question with a question. "Why are you trying to entrap me?" he asks them. "Show me the coin you pay the tax with." When they do, he simply points out that the coin already belongs to Caesar since it has his face and name stamped on it, and he gives them one of the great nonanswers of all time: "Well then, pay Caesar what belongs to him, and pay God what belongs to God." It is the first of a series of skillful parries to his enemies' thrusts, all of which are designed by Jesus to deny the authorities any solid grounds for proceeding against him. Like Thomas More, he is walking a legal tightrope, trying to insure that the case they ultimately bring against him will have to be a trumped-up one. Accordingly, no interpreter should try to prove anything by this passage other than that Jesus was a consummate fox. In particular, no preacher in his or her right mind should ever think of trying to squeeze a sermon on church and state out of it. This is a masterful piece of waffling, not a treatise on the sacred versus the secular; it is not cool theology but the crafty avoidance of hot pursuit. The wise expositor, therefore, will stress its relevance to judgment in general and to the passion in particular—and let it go at that.

The Pharisees' disciples then retire in amazement at Jesus' debating skill, and a fresh team of tempters—the Sadducees (Matt. 22:23-33; Aland no. 281)—come on the field to have a crack at him with a parable of their own. Since, unlike the Pharisees, they deny the notion of a resurrection at the last day—and since Jesus has already made resurrection from the dead the hallmark of his messianic claim—they try to kill two birds (Jesus *and* the Pharisees) with one stone. They tell a story about seven brothers, each of whom successively marries the same woman in order to perpetuate the family line of the brother who predeceased him; then they ask, "To which of the seven will she be married in the resurrection?" Once again, though, Jesus outfoxes the opposition. He simply asserts that the resurrection is a whole new ballgame to which the present rules of marriage do not apply; but then he goes on to prove, by what to modern ears sounds like narrow reasoning indeed, that even the Torah proves there is a resurrection. Since God is the God of Abraham, Isaac, and Jacob, he argues—and since those three patriarchs were not all alive at the same time on earth—therefore, in order for God to be their God, they must all be alive together in some other-than-earthly state, namely, the resurrection. Q.E.D. Once again, I enter a plea for no irrelevant commentaries. Jesus is not talking about the theology of Holy Matrimony here; he is not even talking about what he means by resurrection. Resurrection, for him, is a hot subject, inseparable from his own impending death. It is simply wrongheaded to try to make serious resurrection theology out of what is, at bottom, just a fencing match with cold-blooded doctrine-choppers. The real purpose of the passage, like the purpose of Jesus' argument, is to build up tension in anticipation of his passion, not to answer theological posers.

Next, after yet more astonishment at his cleverness on the part of the people, the Pharisees come back for another round of efforts at entrapment (Matt. 22:34-40; Aland no. 282). They are delighted, of course, at Jesus' silencing of the Sadducees; but their real hope is presumably to get him to continue playing too-clever-by-half games with the Torah. If he was willing to do that kind of fine slicing with Abraham, Isaac, and Jacob, they reason, maybe they can corner him into shaving a few points off a really important part of the Law. So they ask him: "Teacher, which is the great commandment in the Torah?" It is not entirely clear what they expected him to answer. Perhaps they were hoping for one of those sermon-on-the-mountish reinterpretations of his ("You have heard it said by them of old . . . but *I* tell you") that would lead him out onto the thin ice of his own *exousía*. Perhaps not. In any case, Jesus outfoxes them yet again, this time simply by quoting Deut. 6:5 and Lev. 19:18 (about loving God and neighbor) and adding what the Pharisees presumably believe anyway, namely, "On these two commandments hang all the Law and the Prophets." Once more, he is just too fast for them.

Mark notes at this point (Matthew and Luke do so a bit later on) that, "after that, no one dared to ask him any more questions." Jesus, however, now executes a remarkable turn: as if to exasperate his now silent adversaries, he abruptly stops diving for intellectual cover and asks a trick question himself. It is almost as if the fox has found the hunt a disappointment and now comes out, waves at the hounds, and shouts, "Over here!" With the Pharisees still gathered in front of him (Matt. 22:41-46; Aland no. 283), he says to them "What do you think about the Messiah? Whose son is he?" They answer, predictably enough, "The son of David" — echoing the traditional belief that the Messiah would be, among other things, an earthly monarch in the Davidic line. But Jesus has yet another rabbinical-style gambit up his sleeve. Cleverly raising the subject of messianic *exousía,* but giving them no grounds for accusing him of actually making a personal claim to it, he asks them, "How is it then that David, inspired by the Spirit, calls the Messiah his Lord?" For good measure, he even quotes them a proof text, Ps. 110:1: "The Lord said to my lord, sit on my right hand, till I put your enemies under your feet." (A bit of background here: in the Hebrew, the first "Lord" is *YHWH,* the tetragrammaton, the sacred Name of God; the second "lord" is the word *adonai,* which can apply to others as well as God. But since both words were pronounced as *adonai* by custom [the tetragrammaton was never spoken], Jesus is relying here not only on the obvious fact that a king's descendant cannot properly be called his lord [small *l*], but also on the aural coincidence by which the sacred name "Lord" seems to be uttered twice.) Jesus does not, of course, press the latter point. He just leaves the poser as a poser and says nothing more. And so the question-and-answer phase of this first section comes to an end as a shutout: the score is Jesus, four, authorities, zero.

Finally though, with all his pursuers effectively thrown off, Jesus apparently decides that the time for foxiness is over and the time for passion is at hand. The head of steam now starts to blow off. What follows (Matt. 23:1-36; Aland no. 284) is a diatribe against the hypocrisy of the scribes and Pharisees. He has had enough of their insidious pussyfooting: he goes on the attack against them openly. The passage is long, and I do not choose to comment on it in detail. Instead, let me make just two general observations. First, I want you to note that it is strongly, if not viciously, *ad hominem.* Jesus goes after these authorities personally, finding fault after specific fault with their stewardship of the mystery of God. Once again, this is white-hot, human anger on Jesus' part, not calm analysis. But second—precisely because the vehemence of his attack invites not only his immediate hearers but his later expositors to take every word seriously—I want to issue a caveat to preachers. We should be on our guard against the temptation to make abstract ethics out of this passage. Jesus is not doing moral theology here—not giving a lecture on assorted topics such as oaths or the relationship between ritual and righteousness. Rather, he is castigating blind guides and blind fools—compulsive winners who live only by their wisdom and who cannot trust the losing, dying grace, the divine foolishness by which alone God offers salvation to the world. He is a furious Messiah whose messiahship has been rejected by the very people who, in any proper scheme of things, ought to have been the ones to acknowledge it. So he deliberately gives them no quarter. He simply roars on until he runs out of anger and turns, suddenly but with utter realism, to pity. It is another case of sovereign grace speaking in the thick of judgment. Watch how he juxtaposes the two in the last few verses of the passage (Matt. 23:34-39).

He begins his peroration with a wrathful judgment: "Therefore I send you prophets and wise men and scribes, some of whom you will kill and crucify . . . that upon you may come all the righteous blood shed on earth, from the blood of innocent Abel to the blood of Zechariah the son of Barachiah, whom you murdered between the sanctuary and the altar. Truly, I say to you, all this will come upon this generation." But then he goes on without a break into the gracious lament over the city and its inhabitants: "O Jerusalem, Jerusalem, killing the prophets and stoning those who are sent to you! How often would I have gathered your children together as a hen gathers her chicks under her wings, and you would not! Behold, your home is cut off from you. For I tell you, you will not see me again, until you say, 'Blessed is he who comes in the name of the Lord.'"

It is a stunning ending. For the thirty-three verses of his diatribe just prior to the words quoted in the preceding paragraph, he left himself out of the picture: the word *I (egō)* was not mentioned once. But from verse 34 on, he returns forcefully to the solemn exercise of his own unique authority—of the *exousía* that will manifest itself finally in his dying and rising. The whole series of utterly personal proclamations cited above now burst forth: "*I* send"; "Amen, *I* say to you"; "How often would *I* have gathered"; "*I* tell you"; "You will not see *me*." He has, in short, brought them, and us, back to the center he never left—to the death and resurrection he has been foretelling ever since the feeding of the five thousand. It is the sovereignty of the passion all over again—the triumph of the grace that works only in the last, the lost, the least, the little, and the dead.

And as if to underscore that fact, Mark and Luke include at this point, as a kind of dying fall, the quiet passage about the Widow's Mite (Mark 12:41-44; Luke 21:1-4; Aland no. 286). Jesus, apparently exhausted by his own vehemence, sits down opposite the treasury and looks at the scene over which he has just pronounced judgment by grace. He sees many rich people putting in large sums, but his eye fastens only on a poor widow who puts in two copper coins. Calling his disciples, he says to them, "Amen, I say to you [one further, mild exercise of his *exousía*], this poor widow has put in more than all those who are contributing to the treasury. For they all contributed out of their abundance, but she out of her lack has put in everything she had, her whole life *(bíon)*." The Widow's Mite, therefore, is another acted parable (in this case, an action by someone else) that Jesus chooses to hold up as an authentic manifestation of the mystery of salvation-through-loss of which he himself is the ultimate sacrament. There is no balm in this Gilead of winners, he says in effect; there is no physician in this whole city, even though it is hell-bent on saving its life. There is at this moment before judgment only the divine Physician himself—the wounded Surgeon who will shortly die for the city and the world—and one little old lady who, in her lack, is the sign of the only healing there is.

So much for the first of the two stage-setting sections with which I promised to deal. Let me take a slightly different tack on the second (the so-called synoptic apocalypse) and give you a table of contents for the whole before touching on the parts. Its several pericopes are as follows: the Prediction of the Destruction of the Temple (Aland no. 287); the Signs of the Parousia and of the Consummation of the Age (Aland no. 288); the Coming Persecutions (Aland no. 289); the Desolating Sacrilege (Aland no. 290); False Christs and False Prophets (Aland no. 291); and the Coming of the Son of Man (Aland no. 292).

The thread I choose to follow through all of these is the

same one I have been following all along, namely, judgment by grace—the cross and the empty tomb as God's ultimate, vindicating sentence on the whole world. However much Jesus may be using conventional, end-of-the-age imagery here, he is proclaiming that his own end in his death and resurrection is the key to it all. I am not about to maintain, of course, that Jesus can be interpreted as literally saying what some commentators have tried to say, namely, that his passion and death are all there is to his *parousía,* or second coming. He was too clearly speaking of an end beyond the next few days for such an interpretation to hold water. But he does, I think, radically refigure that ultimate end by making himself, dead and risen, the cornerstone of it. Watch.

As Jesus leaves the temple, his disciples come to him (Matt. 24:1-2 and parallels) pointing out, like a group of sightseers, the splendor of the buildings of the temple. But he answers them, "Amen, I say to you [once again, a solemn expression of his own *exousía*], there will not be left here one stone upon another. . . ." As they often do, the disciples are simply covering their confusion with small talk. They sense something darkly mysterious about him, and rather than face it, they try their best to get off the subject. Jesus, though, refuses to be deflected by them. He has just mourned over both the city and the temple. He has seen, in the light of his own approaching end, the end of the entire present dispensation. And he has seen the unfaith that will preclude any saving participation in that end on the part of those who reject him. But he is not about to stop placing himself, in his death and resurrection, in the center of the picture. (This passage, incidentally, needs to be read in connection with the rending of the curtain of the temple at Jesus' death—Matt. 27:51 and parallels—recorded by all three synoptics. Strange as that phenomenon may be, the Gospel writers obviously report it as a corroboration not only of Jesus' predictions of the end of the city and the temple, but also of all of his eschatological pronouncements.)

The subject of the end having been raised, however, and the centrality to it of Jesus himself having been adumbrated, the disciples at last work up the nerve to bring up both subjects—but only in terms of their own, unreconstructedly interventionist eschatological thinking. Coming to Jesus as he sits quietly by himself on the Mount of Olives, they ask him the one question that seems to them important. "Tell us," they say (Matt. 24:3), "when will this be, and what will be the sign (*sēmeion,* sign, the most common Gospel word for 'miracle') of your coming (*parousías,* presence) and of the consummation of the age (*synteleías tou aiōnos*)?" Jesus' answer to this question needs close scrutiny. He does indeed go on to list many signs of the end; but not before he warns the disciples against those who will lead them astray by claiming to be merely plausible messiahs — to be, in other words, right-handed, problem-solving saviors rather than left-handed, problem-sharing ones.

The text, I think, bears this out. The rest of this apocalyptic discourse, taken in its proper Holy Week context, is not the interventionist scenario it first seems. Rather, it is a proclamation of tribulations and death as the true signs of the end—a declaration that the real sacrament of the consummation is *the world's passion as it is taken up in Jesus' passion.* What follows here is not simply an apocalyptic catalogue of woes to be visited on the recalcitrant; it is a picture of the dying/rising Savior reigning in the midst of universal shipwreck. Jesus tells his disciples that they will hear of wars and rumors of wars. But they are not to be alarmed: these things, he says in effect, are simply the way he does business. He saves the world *in* its death, not out of it; therefore the very things that look like a judgmental end to be dreaded will in fact be sacramental signs of the gracious end God has always had in mind. For the real end, the genuine consummation *(syntéleia),* will not be something that supervenes from elsewhere on a disaster from which history must be rescued; it will be something that rises out of the very disaster of history by the power of Jesus' resurrection. He tells them, therefore, that even when they see all these signs of the end, the end itself is not yet. Redemption, he insists, involves neither the rejection of the world in its folly nor the remedying of that folly by right-handed intervention. It consists in letting the folly go all the way into death and then bringing resurrection out of that death.

There is a lesson here for the church as well as the world. Too often, the church preaches resurrection but effectively denies the death out of which alone the grace of resurrection proceeds. Its cure of choice, for its own ills or for the world's, is not death but simply more doomed living. The church, for example, will keep sinners (the morally dead) in its midst only as long as they do not presume to look dead—only as long as they can manage to make themselves seem morally alive. Moreover, ecclesiastical institutions are no more capable of accepting death for themselves than they are of tolerating it in their members. Like all other institutions, they cannot even conceive of going out of business for the sake of grace: given a choice of laying down their corporate lives for a friend or cutting off the friend at the knees, they almost invariably spare themselves the axe. Worst of all, when the church speaks to the world, it perpetuates the same false system of salvation. It is clearly heard as saying that the world can be saved only by getting its act together. But besides being false, that is an utterly unrealistic apologetic. For everyone knows perfectly well that the world never has gotten its act together and never will— that disaster has been the hallmark of its history—and that if there is no one who can save it *in* its disasters, there is no one who can save it. And therefore when the church comes to the world mouthing the hot air that the future is amenable to reform—that the kingdom can be built here by plausible devices, by something other than the mystery of the passion — the church convinces no one. Murphy's Law *vincit omnia:* late or soon, the world is going down the drain; only a Savior who is willing to work at the bottom of the drain can redeem it. The world does indeed have a future and the church alone has that future to proclaim. But that future is neither pie on earth nor pie in the sky. It is resurrection from the dead — and without death, there can be no resurrection.

In the rest of the synoptic apocalypse, Jesus drums on with

the same insistent beat. He tells the disciples (Matt. 24:9-14 and parallels; Aland no. 289) that they, as well as the world, will be caught up in his passion and death. Nothing will go right or come out right. The authentic sign of his *parousía*— the one, effective sacrament to the mystery of his redemption —will be their enduring to the end in the unrightness of it all: Jerusalem will fall, the temple will be profaned, the Jewish nation will be scattered (Matt. 24:15-22 and parallels; Aland no. 290), and "there will be great tribulation, such as has not been seen from the beginning of the world until now, no, nor ever will be." But then he adds what I think is a pregnant verse: "And if those days had not been cut short, no human being would be saved; but for the sake of the elect, whom he chose [Mark 13:20 adds this last phrase], he has cut short the days."

Think about that. I have no doubt that in the minds of Jesus' disciples at the time—and very likely in Jesus' mind too —those words constituted a reference to the duration of the specific passion of Israel he was talking about: to the cutting short, the ending of that passion by the merciful action of God. But I think it also has a wider meaning—one that is borne out not only in the Gospels themselves but in the wider context of the Bible as a whole: the "cutting short of the days" is ultimately a reference to death itself. First of all, Jesus' passion in the Gospels is cut short only by death. It leads not to some ameliorative action—not to a coming down from the cross— but to nothing. It is only after that nothing that the saving resurrection occurs. Second, though, Christians (beginning with Paul) have commonly interpreted Adam and Eve's expulsion from Eden (and the concomitant sequestering of the Tree of Life) as meaning that death came into the world not simply as a punishment for sin but as a *preparatio evangelica,* a merciful provision. For not only does death cut short sin in our present, fallen lives; it also becomes, in the Good News of Jesus' death, the sole condition of our being raised to newness of life by the power of his resurrection. All our days have been cut short, therefore: the world's, Jerusalem's, yours, and mine. For the sake of saving whom he will, he has removed the threat of no salvation from every human being (*pása sarx,* all flesh) by making death the universal safe harbor.

And so Jesus returns to the theme with which he began the synoptic apocalypse. "Then if anyone says to you," he tells the disciples (Matt. 24:23-28 and parallels; Aland no. 291), "'Lo, here is the Christ!' or 'There he is!' do not believe it. For false Christs and false prophets will arise and show great signs and wonders [marvelous, and no doubt ameliorative, programs], so as to lead astray, if possible, even the elect." The warning is as necessary now as it was then, because "the elect" have been, and still are, regularly led astray. I am not about to get into a discussion of the mischief wrought throughout the history of Christian theology by efforts to identify the elect on some moral or spiritual basis. I want only to point out that in many of the New Testament uses of the word (the Greek is *eklektoí*), it is simply an alternative way of of referring to the church (see, for example, 2 Tim. 2:10; 1 Pet. 1:1; 2 John 1, 13). Accordingly, I am disposed to think that Jesus' warning in this passage has a singular relevance to the church. For what is the church? It is not, in any sound theology, an exclusive club of the saved. It is rather the elect sign, the chosen sacrament of the salvation wrought by Jesus for the whole world. It is, in short, catholic. And yet what has this elect sign, this sacrament of catholicity, so often done? It has acted as if *it* were the salvation of the world and as if its members were the sum total of the saved. It has risen up like a false Christ and stipulated the spiritual signs and wonders by which it thinks the kingdom can be brought in. It has said that Jesus is only in the correct, or the good, or the spiritual. It has even implied that he is the sole property of the ecclesiastical institution itself.

But against all that, Jesus says, "Don't believe it" (Matt. 24:26). "For as the lightning comes from the east and shines as far as the west, so will the coming (*parousía*) of the Son of man be: wherever the body is, there the eagles will be gathered together" (verse 27). Once again, the imagery is pregnant. Not only does Jesus' reference to the simultaneous and universal presence of lightning throughout the whole sky clearly underscore the "presence" aspect of his *parousía* (Jesus does not *arrive somewhere* to announce the end of the world, he is already *present everywhere* in the very fact of that end); his use of the imagery of the body and the eagles even more clearly underscores the centrality of his death to consummation of the world. For what are eagles? They are, of course, birds of prey, accipiters. But since Jesus is presumably referring to them here as birds of carrion (like vultures), they appear in this imagery as accepters of death, as feeders upon death. They are, in other words, an image of faith—of faith in the death of Jesus that is the only touchstone of salvation. What the verse means to me, therefore, is that since the dead Jesus is present in all deaths, all those who trust—who by faith accept him in that *parousía*—will be saved. Accordingly, the only test of the church's own fidelity is whether it is being true or false to the Good News of his death and resurrection. That was its first and only apostolic proclamation, and that proclamation remains its only real claim to catholicity. If the church preaches faith in anything other than the resurrection—if it gives so much as the impression that anything else, be it political action, moral achievement, or spiritual proficiency, can save the world—it becomes just one more false, parochial prophet leading the world away from the catholic *parousía* of Christ in the universal death of history.

Fittingly enough, it is in the very darkness of that proclamation that Jesus begins the finale of the synoptic apocalypse (Matt. 24:29-31 and parallels; Aland no. 292). Let me set it forth in full for you, giving my interpretation as I go. *"Immediately after the tribulation of those days,"* he says, *"the sun will be darkened and the moon will not give its light and the stars will fall from heaven and the powers of the heavens will be unsettled."* This is the hour of grace, the moment before the general resurrection when a whole dead world lies still—when all the successes that could never save it and all the failures it could never undo have gone down into the silence of Jesus' death. *"And then the sign of the Son of man will appear in heaven and all the tribes of the earth will mourn."* This is the hour of judgment, the moment of the resurrection when the whole world receives its new life out of death. And it is also the moment of hell, when all those who find they can no longer return to their old lives of estrangement foolishly mourn their loss of nothing and refuse to accept the only reality there is. *"And they will see the Son of man coming on the clouds of heaven with power and great glory; and he will send out his angels with a loud trumpet and they will gather his elect from the four winds, from one end of heaven to the other."*

This, at last, is the end: the triumph of the acceptance that is heaven and the catastrophe of the rejection that is hell. And the only difference between the two is faith. No evil deeds are judged, because the whole world was dead to the law by the body of Christ (Rom. 7:4). And no good deeds are required, for Christ is the end of the law so that everyone who believes may be justified (Rom. 10:4). Judgment falls only on those who refuse to believe there is no judgment—who choose to stand before a Judge who no longer has any records and take their stand on a life that no longer exists.

And heaven? Heaven is the gift everyone always had by the death of the Lamb slain from the foundation of the world (Rev. 13:8, NIV, KJV). All it ever took to enjoy it was trust.

CHAPTER ELEVEN

The Flood of Judgment by Mercy

The Fig Tree; the Flood;
the Faithful Servant and the Bad Servant

All three synoptic Gospels agree in placing the parable of the Fig Tree (Matt. 24:32-36 and parallels; Aland no. 293) right after the eschatological discourses we have just dealt with, thus making it a kind of coda to the synoptic apocalypse. But beyond that point, they differ considerably as to how they tie things up before starting the passion narrative (at Matt. 26; Mark 14; Luke 22). Luke's conclusion is brief: he ends (Luke 21:34-36; Aland no. 295) with Jesus' warning not to be weighed down with dissipation and the cares of this life, but rather to "watch at all times." Mark's ending is even briefer (Mark 13:33), but he follows it up with a pruned-down version (in Aland, no. 294) of the parable of the Talents/Coins with which I have already dealt. Matthew, however, is in no such rush to get off the subject of eschatology: not only does he include the Fig Tree, the Flood, and the Two Servants in chapter 24; he devotes the whole of chapter 25 to three more parables of judgment: the Ten Virgins, the Talents, and the Great Judgment. Accordingly, since all of these remaining parables will now appear sequentially in Matthew, I choose to follow that Gospel from here on.

First, then, the parable of the Fig Tree. "Learn the lesson (*parabolên,* parable) of the fig tree," Jesus says, wrapping up everything he has been saying about the end and the signs of

143

the *parousía* of the Son of man: "when its branches become green and tender, and it puts forth leaves, you know that summer is near. So also, when you see all these things, you know that he is at the very door *(engýs estin epí thýrais)*. As I read these words, they corroborate the notion I put forth in the previous chapter, namely, that the apocalyptic end-events (wars, persecutions, earthquakes, etc.) are not just warm-up acts for a coming of Christ that will supersede them, but *that very coming itself,* under the form of death. For just as the leaves of springtime are not mere advertisements for summer, but the very engines that will enable the plant to do summer's work, so with the tribulation and death at the consummation. Those things do not merely represent the passion and death of Christ; they *are* his passion and death already knocking at the world's door for acceptance by faith. They are, as I have said, not mere signs but genuine sacraments, real presences of the mystery of redemption.

I am aware you may think that forced, but it is not. If it bothers you, it does so chiefly because of the unfortunate habit of referring to the the *parousía* of Jesus as his "second coming." Let me say again, therefore, that our usual notion of Jesus' coming to the world—or even of the coming of the kingdom—is not only theologically suspect but biblically unsound. For "coming" inevitably carries with it the implication of "not here yet"—which, of course, simply will not wash in the case of the Word who became incarnate in Jesus. The Word did not "show up" in a world from which he was previously absent; he was here all along. In particular, though, the notion of "showing up" will not wash in the case of the *parousía.* For the incarnate Lord who will manifest himself at the end of history is none other than the Lamb slain from the foundation of the world. The mystery of his reconciliation of the world has been present in it from the start; no manifestation of that mystery—not even his *parousía* at the end—is a merely future event. The resurrection of the dead is not stuck out there in traffic on the thruway trying to get to our house. The judgment is not in a phone booth somewhere struggling to make a connection. And the ultimate re-creation of all things in heaven and earth is not in the mail, waiting for the celestial post office to get its act together. All those things are present, now and always, because the incarnate Word is present, now and always, *in the world's mortality*. We are baptized into those things by being baptized in Jesus' death. We feast upon those things by partaking of the power of Jesus' resurrection in a eucharistic meal that presents him as dead—in his body broken and blood shed. And we—and the whole world, Christian or not—live every second of our lives in the very presence of the judgment by resurrection from the dead that vindicates us all.

As we normally conceive of "coming," therefore, Jesus is not coming at all; he is here. And Scripture bears that out. When Jesus announces the kingdom (for example, Mark 1:15), he says it "has drawn near" (*ēngiken,* a verb in the perfect tense, signifying an already accomplished action standing as a present reality). Moreover, in this parable of the Fig Tree, he says, "when you see all these things, you know he is near, at the door" *(engýs estin epí thýrais)* —meaning, of course, that he is *here at the house,* not across town or down the block. And when Jesus uses the word *thýrais,* "doors," he reinforces that note of presence mightily. In Rev. 3:20 he says, "Behold, I stand at the door *(thýran)* and knock"—which means that he is present to us at every moment, waiting only for us to acknowledge his presence and let him in by faith. But above all, Jesus himself *is* the door. In John 10, where he sets himself forth as the Good Shepherd who lays down his life for the sheep, he says, "I am the door *(thýra);* if anyone enters by me, he will be saved and will go in and out and find pasture" (John 10:9). In this ultimate image, therefore, Jesus stunningly reverses all our preconceptions about coming: he does not come to us—does not enter our lives—by some kind of divine locomotion; instead, *he* stands still—in his own death on the cross and in his constant presence in all deaths—and *we* come to him. Or, to put it in T. S. Eliot's words, Jesus' death is the "still point of the turning world": whenever we come in faith to our own death, we find it to be that same "still point," the abiding Door to resurrection and life.

All of which is borne out by the words that follow in the parable of the Fig Tree: "Amen, I say to you, this generation shall not pass away till all these things take place. Heaven and earth will pass away, but my words will not pass away" (Matt. 24:34-35). If you grapple with that text on the basis of a mere second-coming interpretation, you only indulge yourself in silly speculations about whether Jesus thought he was coming back in fifty days, fourteen months, six years, or two millennia—speculations, please note, that no one has any way of confirming or denying, and that Jesus himself specifically discourages in the immediately following verse. But if you grapple with it in terms of the *parousía* as his *having already come*—as the sacramental manifestation of a kingdom already here, already fully operative in *all* the acts of his ministry, past, present, or future—it lights up brilliantly. Because then you can take the text, "this generation shall not pass away *till all these things be fulfilled*," as referring either to his death-resurrection or to his second coming — on the ground that his *parousía* is just as fully manifested by the former as by the latter. Which, fascinatingly enough, simply lands you right back at what sound Christian doctrine has always insisted on, namely, that the death and resurrection of Jesus are nothing less than *the whole story*—the full, perfect, and sufficient sacrifice, oblation, and satisfaction for the sins of the whole world. What "this generation" saw fulfilled a mere two days later, therefore, was indeed the fulfillment of all things. They couldn't possibly have seen more, even if they could have lasted a million years. Even at the clap of doom, the job they would see done then would be nothing more and nothing less than the job they were about to see done now: some different special effects, perhaps, but the same age-long business of grace raising the dead.

And with that, the concluding verse of the parable lights up as well. All through the illustration of the Fig Tree so far, Jesus has been talking of present, knowable manifestations of his *parousía*—of signs that, like the tender leaves of the fig tree, are sacramental manifestations of the eternal summer, not just extrinsic advertisements for it. Now though, in Matt. 24:36, he allows himself one reference to the *parousía* as a future event—to his "coming" at the end of history as the final sacrament of his presence all along: "But of that day and hour no one knows, not even the angels of heaven, nor the Son, but the Father only." Do you see? He contrasts *this generation,* which will shortly see all there is to see in his death and resurrection, with *that day,* on which the whole world will finally see it all as well. He contrasts faith in the mystery hidden in his dying and rising with the open vision of that mystery at the end of time. And as I said, he has only one thing to say on the subject: since no one, not even he, knows beans about the timing of that day, nothing counts now but our trust that, in him, everything is already fulfilled. The summer is at hand *(engýs);* we don't have to do anything but believe it. We will all get a gorgeous tan in the due season; all we have to do now is be sure we can find the bikini of faith—the light, free-and-easy, postage-stamp-size garment of acceptance of his acceptance—that will expose us to as much of the Sun as possible.

It is just this notion of faith, as I see it, that is picked up in the next parable, Jesus' eschatological recapitulation of the tale of Noah and the Flood (Matt. 24:37-44; Aland no. 296). The true scriptural function of the story of Noah is more often than not obscured by interpretations that pay attention only to its judgmental aspects. It is not an account of the wrath of God at the disaster of human history; it is the proclamation of God's mercy as God's ultimate way of dealing with sin. The principal symbolic element that gives it a preeminent place in the Scriptures is not the flood at its beginning but the rainbow at the end. God, after forty days' murderous exercise of his anger over sin, hangs up his judgmental artillery as a sign of his solemn determination to exercise mercy instead. He "sets his bow in the clouds"—sets, that is, a perennial, natural sign of remission and peace—as a witness to the covenant of grace that constitutes his ultimate relationship to the world. Even as early as Gen. 6–9, therefore, the sovereignty of grace over judgment is clearly intimated in Scripture.

More than that, though, Noah himself becomes one of the first great signs of faith—even before Abraham, the father of faith, appears on the scene. In Heb. 11:7, the author makes faith the touchstone of the flood: "By faith *(pístei)* Noah, being warned by God concerning the events as yet unseen, took heed and constructed an ark for the saving *(sōtērían*, salvation) of his household; by this he condemned the world and became an heir of the righteousness that comes by faith *(katá pístin)*." Moreover, Noah's faith is precisely a trust in the operation of God in disaster—the very thing Jesus has been talking about all through the synoptic apocalypse. All of which Jesus picks up when he chooses the Flood as a parable of the *parousía,* of the *presence in disaster* of the Son of man. "As were the days of Noah," Jesus begins, "so will be the coming *(parousía)* of the Son of man. For as in those days before the flood they were eating and drinking, marrying and giving in marriage, until the day when Noah entered into the ark, and they did not know until the flood came and swept them away, so will be the coming *(parousía* again) of the Son of man."

Yet once more, the theme I have been trying to develop fairly leaps from the text. On the one hand, the eating, drinking, and marrying that Jesus adduces are stand-ins for all the plausible, winning, life-saving activities by which the human race loses its life; on the other hand, the faithful obedience of Noah is a stand-in for the losing and death by which alone our life is saved. It is not that Noah is excused from the flood; it is that he rides it out by faith (losing everything but his own skin and his immediate family) and finds, in the disaster itself, the grace of God. Indeed, in 1 Pet. 3:18-22, the author of that epistle not only stresses this note of salvation by disaster (the very waters that killed the disobedient were the ones that bore up the ark, saving the eight souls in it); he also goes on to tie the imagery of the flood to the waters of baptism in which we both die with Christ and rise with Christ. (Yes, Virginia, that *is* a long reach; but since I didn't think it up, I feel no compunction about putting it before you. At the very least, it will tell you why baptistries in medieval churches had *eight* sides.)

But above all, what leaps most clearly from Jesus' parable of the Flood is the centrality of faith to the mystery of the *parousía*. Again and again, he insists that his coming is not a matter of knowledge (Matt. 24:39, 42, 43: "they" did not know; "you" do not know; "the householder" does not know). The way God runs the world, no one will ever *know* anything but that things are a mess. Some may be taken and some left, but none of us, any more than Noah, is excused from the passion that is history. The incidentals of our involvement in the disaster may vary, but the disaster remains the chosen place of his *parousía*. "Watch, therefore," Jesus says (Matt. 24:42); and "be ready" (verse 44). Whatever it may be that we know or think we know—whatever it is that we can contrive to do or to avoid—none of it does anything but drive us closer to the rocks year by year. But what we are invited to watch for and be ready for—what we are invited *now* to wait for in faith— is the Savior who reigns in the midst of the rocks, who is himself the Stone of Stumbling and the Rock of Offense, and who, if we will only believe, is the Cornerstone of the new creation.

And that brings us at last to Matthew's ending of the synoptic apocalypse: the parable of the Faithful Servant and the Bad Servant (Matt. 24:45-51 and parallels; Aland no. 297). I know I have tried your patience with all my harping on faith as the key to both the *parousía* and the judgment, but this is no time to stop. We are all of us so enthralled by a moralistic approach to the Gospel that no effort to break its hold on us can ever be too much; and this parable, on its very face, is an example of the antimoralism of Scripture too perfect to miss. For in spite of the tens of thousands of sermons that have expounded it as proclaiming reward for the good and punishment for the bad, it never once identifies the rewarded servant as good, only as faithful *(pistós)* and wise *(phrónimos)*.

It cannot be said too often that in the New Testament, the opposite of sin is not virtue, it is faith. Not only does Paul say as much in Rom. 14:23: "All that is not of faith is sin"; his

THE PARABLES OF JUDGMENT

endless insistence that salvation is not by the works of the law but by grace through faith (not to mention Jesus' constant habit of making prodigals, unjust stewards, tax collectors, and sinners into heroes) bears witness to the fact that our morals have nothing to do with either our salvation or our damnation. We are saved only because God, immorally, has accepted us while we are yet sinners; and we are damned only if we stupidly (that is, as neither faithful nor wise) insist on rejecting that acceptance by unbelief. Nothing else whatsoever enters into the case.

Yes, Virginia? No, Virginia, that is not overstated. I know you are dying to get me to qualify it, but I am not going to. What's that? You don't want me to qualify it? You only want me to add that for those who truly believe, good behavior will inevitably spring forth out of gratitude for grace? Well, Virginia, it may come as a surprise to you, but I refuse to do that either. Because I suspect you of being a closet moralist. You protest that you are not? I shall prove that you are.

Take Harry. Make him an adulterer who believes. Is he saved? Yes. Is he saved because he stopped shacking up? No. He is saved by trusting the free grace of Jesus' death and resurrection, no questions asked. If there were no Jesus, Harry could stop shacking up till the cows came home and still not be saved. It's Jesus, therefore, who makes all the difference, not Harry's avoidance of shacks.

But to come to your pet point, take Harry again. Make him a believing adulterer who has for three years last past not cheated on his wife. But then slip him back between the motel sheets for another fling. What are you going to say now? That he never really believed? Why? He was saved just saying yes to Jesus, not by the amount of teeth clenching he put into it, or by the integrity of the reforms he tacked onto it. Or do you want to say that he has undone his previous acceptance by subsequent rejection and so has blown his chances by kicking God in the head? Why? The Word became incarnate for the express purpose of being kicked in the head. In fact, Jesus got kicked so hard he ended up with a dead brain—which is about as close as you can get to a God who doesn't even think about sin, let alone have problems with it. What are you trying to do? Turn the God who cancelled the handwriting against us into a welsher who keeps a black list in his pocket for sinners whose timing was no good—who sinned after faith instead of only before it? Turn faith into some kind of work-in-progress which, if interrupted, gets a rejection slip? I will tell you what you are trying to do, Virginia. You are trying to send the publican back to the temple with the Pharisee's speech on his lips. You are trying to turn the Good News of grace into the bad news of law. *You are trying to make an honest man out of God.* And it is driving you straight up the wall, because God is not an honest man. God is a crook (I knew I should have picked up on the word thief, *kléptes,* in the parable of the Flood). He comes like a thief (Rev. 3:3); he cheats on the accounts and then congratulates himself for being unjust (Luke 16:1-8); and he is such a dishonest judge that he pronounces favorable judgment on the world just because it is a pain in the neck (Luke 18:1-8). And you know why you are trying to turn him into an honest man like that? Because you are disgusted at the ungodly indiscriminateness of accepting every last sinner in the world without checking out even a single one beforehand. Because you are scared witless at your entirely correct suspicion that the situation is even worse than you thought—that God is so sure of his acceptance of us in Jesus that he doesn't even put our *faith* to the test. Oh, I know. You say you believe that. You pray, "Lead us not into temptation (*peirasmós,* test, trial)." But when push comes to shove, you want a nasty-nice little judge who will keep crimes against faith off the streets. But God won't even do that, Virginia. Unfaith is its own punishment. All God ever does is confirm the stupid sentence of alienation it pronounces on itself; all he ever condemns are people who want to be more respectable than he is.

But enough. The best part of it all is that even your insistence on being a moralistic turkey (or even mine on flying off the handle) doesn't matter. Nothing ever matters—nothing ever will matter—but faith. Back to the parable.

"Blessed (*makários,* happy) is that servant," Jesus says, praising the wisdom of waiting in faith, "whom his master (*kýrios,* lord) when he comes will find so doing. Amen, I say to you, he will set him over all his possessions" (Matt. 24:46-47). Salvation is not a matter of getting a reward that will make up for a rotten deal; it is a matter of entering by faith into the happiness—the hilarity beyond all liking and happening—that has been pounding on our door all along. Oh, admittedly, the deal of life in this world is rotten enough: God in his crooked wisdom has not taken the disasters out of life, he has become our Life in the midst of the disasters. But if we believe that! If we live through the irremovable disasters trusting that every last, bitter twist of fate is nothing but Jesus, Jesus, Jesus—well, that is rather more happiness than anyone could possibly have bargained for here. It is being in a snug harbor all through a stormy voyage. It is being home free all the while we were lost.

And when the Lord comes at the end—when Jesus makes the last, grand sacramentalization of his perennial presence to all of history, when he sets his faithful servants over all his possessions—well, I suppose *then* it will indeed be pie in the sky. But not a new pie, or a pie after a meal of nothing but watery soup and no meat. It will be seconds—and thirds, and thousandths, and billionths—from a pie that was always under the table and from which, by faith, we constantly filched unjust deserts. Mother earth, that dreadful old cook, may have given us no better than we deserved; but our Father in heaven, through our faith in the death and resurrection of Jesus, has been slipping us the ultimate dessert all along.

Which, if you will permit me now to go back to the opening verse of this parable (Matt. 24:45), gives me a way of expanding upon the image of food (*trophé,* nourishment) that Jesus throws out at the start. It is not just that we are happy because we ourselves have, by faith, been feasting all our lives (in the eucharist, in our own passion) on the Bread of Heaven—tasting that the Lord is indeed good; it is that we are happy because we are a church (if we have been faithful to our stewardship) that has been slipping the world the same goodies. The mission of the church is not to be humanity's bad cook, pushing at it the lumpy mashed potatoes of morality or the thin gruel of spiritual uplift; the mission of the church is to be the Lord's own conspirator, sneaking to the world the delectability of grace, the solid chocolate Good News that God, in the end, has a sweet tooth. Our joy as the stewards of the mystery is to have been in on the joke that God is just a big, bad boy. He doesn't really care a fig for teaching the world lessons about what's good for it; he only wants to make it smile.

But what of the unfaithful servant, the bad church? What of the church that wickedly says, "My Lord *chronizei*" — my Lord is making a big mistake here, taking his own sweet time about the serious business of salvation? What of the church that begins to beat its fellow servants' knuckles with the carving knife of ethical requirements and to get drunk on the cheap wine of successful living or the rotgut booze of spiritual achievement? Well, Jesus tells us what: "The Lord of that servant will punish him, and put him with the hypocrites; there men will weep and gnash their teeth" (Matt. 24:48-51). There is indeed a judgment on such a church. But it is precisely a condemnation for its having made a serious business—a tissue of works—out of the divine lark of grace. The wickedness of the church can be one thing and one only: *turning the Good News of Jesus into the bad news of religion.* Christianity is not a religion; it is the announcement, in the death and resurrection of Jesus, of the end ofs religion—of the end of any and all requirements for the salvation of the world. And therefore, when the church preaches anything but faith alone in Jesus, it is an unfaithful church and deserves only to be put with the rest of the world's hypocrites who think they can be saved by passing tests. It is a church that has stopped being funny and happy in the freedom of faith, and has gone dead in its own earnestness.

Is that another long reach, Virginia? I don't think it is; but since I owe you one, call it whatever you like. You and I have had our last run-in; time now to head for the barn.

CHAPTER TWELVE

The End of the Storm (I)

The Wise and Foolish Virgins

It is a commonplace of literary criticism that authors give themselves away in their last chapters. However much they may have allowed themselves a certain latitude of expression during the earlier parts of their work, they do at last tighten their focus and give their readers the crispest possible picture of what they have been trying to say all along. It is with that in mind that I come now to Matt. 25 (Aland nos. 298-300), the final chapter of Jesus' entire corpus of parables. For the three parables that it comprises—the Ten Virgins, the Talents, and the Great Judgment—are indeed the capstone of his teaching. Not only are all of the notes he has previously struck present in them; in addition, those notes are at last harmonized and given their ultimate expression.

Before proceeding to the parables themselves, however, I want to alert you to two of the notes that Jesus singles out for special emphasis. The first is the absence of the main character from the part of the parable that corresponds to our life now. This note of the missing or hidden Lord—of the *Deus absconditus*—has of course been sounded before: the king in the King's Son's Wedding, for example, does not appear at the party until all the guests have made their several responses to his invitation; the lord in the Faithful Servant and the Bad Servant is not only away, but takes his time *(chronízei)* about finally showing up in person. But in these last three parables, the note of absence becomes practically the fulcrum of the judgment *(krísis)* that takes place when the main character finally appears. In the Ten Virgins, the bridegroom delays his coming (the word, again, is the verb *chronízein*); in the Talents, the lord of the servants returns "after a long time"; and in the Great Judgment, the King judges both the sheep and the goats on the basis of what they did to him when he was completely hidden from them "in the least of his brethren."

Accordingly, these parables are about a judgment pronounced on a world from which God, through all its history, was effectively *absent*—or to put it more carefully, was present in a way so mysterious as to constitute, for all practical purposes, an absence. And therefore, insofar as they address themselves to humanity's response to that hidden God—and to that God's judgment of the response—they are not about practical good works. They do not make moral behavior or spiritual achievement the matter of judgment; rather, they base the judgment solely on faith or unfaith in the mystery of the age-long presence-in-absence—the abiding *parousía* under history—of the divine redemption. Obviously, this note of faith in the mystery of grace has been a constant emphasis in all of Jesus' parables so far, and it has certainly been the note I myself have chosen to stress above all others. But in these last parables, it is, quite simply, everything.

The second note I want to alert you to has the same characteristics. It is none other than what I called, at the very beginning of this book, the master principle of interpretation for all the parables of judgment, namely, the principle of inclusion before exclusion—the rule that any characters who are made outsiders at the end of the story must always be shown as insiders at the beginning. It too has been demonstrated many times before. The man without the wedding garment in the King's Son's Wedding was just as much an accepted guest as all the others, bad or good. The servant who hid the coin in a napkin was no less a recipient of his lord's trust, and thus no less a beneficiary of his lord's presence-in-absence, than the other nine. But now Jesus reinforces the principle by three illustrations in a row. All of the ten virgins, wise or foolish, are equally members of the wedding from the start. All three servants who received the talents are fully accepted by their lord. Both the sheep and the goats have lived their entire lives in the full, if hidden, presence of the King in the least of his brethren. Once again, therefore, faith is set forth as the only criterion of judgment. Those who are congratulated at the end are those who believed in the mysterious, vindicating *parousía* of the main character and who lived their lives on the basis of that trust. Those who are condemned are those who did not. It is not the good works of the blessed that saves them, any more than it is the evil deeds of the cursed that damns them. It is only faith or unfaith that matters.

But there is also something else here. In these last parables, the primacy of faith is finally set forth in a way that meets a lurking objection you have probably felt every time I brought it up. That objection, to give it its proper name, was about the danger of quietism. Almost always, when salvation by faith alone is seriously preached, we feel that somehow it has all been made too easy. Assuming, falsely, that faith is simply a kind of intellectual assent to a proposition, we then go on to conclude that the general reaction of the human race to salvation by faith will be an equally intellectual reaction of indifference. We are afraid they will say, "Well, if all the real work of salvation has already been done, and the only thing we have to do is believe it, why should we bother trying to be good, kind, or loving? If the world is saved in spite of its sins, what's to stop us from going right on doing rotten things?"

Since those are two separate questions, let me deal with them in order. The fallacy in the first is precisely the assumption already noted that faith is assent to a proposition. It is not. It is the living out of a trust-relationship with a person. If it were only something in our heads, then we might well conclude that it had no implications for what we might do with our hands or our feet or with any of our other members or faculties. But since nothing is simply in our heads—since we will always, as long as we live, be *doing something*—that is a

156

false conclusion. Therefore a better form of this first question would be, "If he has already done it all for me already, why shouldn't I live as if I trusted him?" If he has made me a member of the Wedding of the Lamb why shouldn't I act as if I am at the party? If he has already reconciled both my wayward self and my equally difficult brother-in-law, or children, or wife, why shouldn't I at least try to act as if I trust him to have done just that and to let his reconciliation govern my actions in those relationships?

Quietism, you see—do-nothingism—is not a viable option. And it is not viable for one simple reason: Jesus' reconciled version of all relationships is the only version that really counts—the only one that in the end will be real at all. When we die, we lose whatever grip we had on our unreconciled version of our lives. And when we rise at the last day, the only grip in which our lives will be held will be the reconciling grip of Jesus' resurrection. He will hold our lives mended, cleaned, and pressed in his hand, and he will show them to his Father. And his Father, seeing the only real you or me there is to see, will say, "Wonderful! Just what I had in mind." He will say over the Word's new creation of us at the last day exactly what he said over the Word's first creation of us on the sixth day: "Very good!"

That is the final answer to quietism. And therefore the best of all possible forms of the first question is, "Since he has already made me new—since there really isn't any of the old me around to get in my way any more—why should I be so stupid as to try to go on living in terms of something that isn't even there?" Faith, you see, is simply taking his word about what really is and trying our best to get all the unreal nonsense out of our lives. Strictly speaking, faith does not save us; *he* does; but because faith, once given, inexorably leads us to try to stop contradicting what he has done, it becomes the only instrument of salvation that we need to lay a hand to.

The second question is likewise based on a fallacy. To ask, "If the world is already saved in spite of its sins, what's to stop people from sinning?" is to misunderstand the nature of sin.

Sin is not something the human race has any choice about. The occasional sin (small *s*), we might manage to stop: some of us might possibly avoid this lie or that adultery. But none of us will ever avoid that trust in ourselves—and that distrust of anyone else—that lies at the root of the world's problems. Those twin falsities of faith in self and unfaith in others are as irremovable by human effort as they are unpardonable by human good will. And therefore if they are ever to be removed or pardoned, it will only be by God's gift. But that gift, please note, stands in no *causal* relationship whatsoever to our responses. It will neither force us to be better nor enable us to go on being worse. It is simply a fact, to be trusted or not as we choose. That it is the only real fact, happens to be true; but that it will strong-arm an unreality-loving world into reversing gears and loving reality is just not in the cards. It is a free gift, and it aims to elicit only a free response of faith. Without constraining anyone or condoning anything, it just hands us a new creation and invites us to live as if we trusted it.

One last note on all three of these parables. Their insistence that the judgment upon faith will be a judgment on faith-in-action, not on faith-with-folded-hands, goes to the heart of the biblical view of history. In the Bible, the course of the world and the course of God's action in it are like an arrow shot toward a target, not like a planet endlessly pursuing an unchanging, circular course. And nowhere is this "linear as opposed to circular" view more manifest than in the biblical notion of judgment. In a "circular" system, there is no possibility of judgment, of history-altering and history-fulfilling *krisis,* happening *from within the system.* The only controlling *parousia* (presence) in the orbit, say, of Mars around the sun is the constant presence of gravitation producing an equally constant repetition of course: Mars is not going anywhere but *around.* If there is a *krisis,* it will have to come from outside the system—from, for example, a collision with an alien body. But in a "linear" system, judgment is built in; *krisis* is the whole point of the system. The target is where the arrow is *going,* and every action in the whole of the arrow's course—the drawing of it from the quiver, the setting of it on the bowstring, the releasing of the bow, and the flight of the arrow through the air—everything, quite literally, is governed by the history-fulfilling judgment of the bull's-eye at the end: it partakes of the nature of that *krísis* at every point.

So it is with the biblical view of history in general, and so it is with Jesus' parables of judgment in particular. Both it and they are about an action going somewhere to happen. They are not about a system of static recurrences in which time goes on forever—where there is always, by the rules of the system, time for a second chance at everything. They do not allow you the luxury of a historical perspective in which a step taken too soon or a move made too late can always be remedied the next time around. Rather, they are about a world in which too early or too late can be crashing, fatal mistakes—in which there is only one chance for anything: one moment to aim the arrow, one brief, high time to make allowances for the crosswind, one critical instant to shoot, and one final judgment, hit or miss, on the entire proceeding. In the Ten Virgins, for example, the bridegroom comes late, the oil of the foolish has run out, the storekeepers' shops are closed, and the door to the marriage feast is shut. In the Talents, the time for doing business is finally over for good. And in the Great Judgment, the day of ministry to the King who lives in the least is gone forever. Just as history is a series of unrepeatable, even unrehearsable performances, so the history of salvation is just one *krísis* after another, with no going back.

These final parables, therefore, give the ultimate lie to the view of faith as intellectual assent to static truths. What God saves by grace through faith is precisely the *dynamic* of history, the once-and-never-again quality of a world he was pleased to make that way. He saves history by history; and at the end, it is history that he brings home smack in the center of the target. Even faith, therefore, is something that must somehow, somewhere be *done*. And if it is left undone . . . , well, there will be a price for that. Though you may not have expected me to say it, I am too much of an orthodox Christian, and too much of a historical realist, to think there is any way of getting hell out of the scriptural account of the final reconciliation. We should not, of course, be too eager to set up our rules for what constitutes the limit, temporal or eternal, of God's patience with unfaith. But these parables say plainly enough that there is a limit and there will one day be a *kairós,* a high time of *krísis,* beyond which the unreal will be allowed no further truck with reality. He wills the eternal picnic to begin. The party poopers do not have forever to go on praying for rain.

On then with the parables themselves. Jesus begins the Ten Virgins (Matt. 25:1-13; Aland no. 298) by harking back to the style of introduction that characterized his earliest parables: "Then the kingdom of heaven shall be likened to ten maidens." The word *then* refers clearly enough to the end, the climactic manifestation of the *parousía* of the Son of man that Jesus has been speaking of just prior to this point. But in joining it to the words "the kingdom of heaven shall be likened to . . . ," he brings his whole parabolic opus to completion. At the beginning of his ministry, in the parables of the kingdom, he proclaimed the mystery of a kingdom already present in this world. In the parables of grace that followed, he proclaimed the device by which that mystery operates, namely, grace working through death and resurrection. Now though, he comes full circle and gives, in the concluding parables of judgment, a series of pictures of how it ultimately triumphs, separating those who accept the mystery in faith from those who, by unfaith, reject his freely given acceptance of them in the resurrection of the dead.

The ten maidens, he says, "took their lamps and went to meet the bridegroom." The image is as charming as it is earnest. Here are ten girls (permit me to make them fourteen-year-olds) on their way, every last one of them, to a party. They are, presumably, tickled to the point of teenage giggliness at their happy prospects. The *krísis* of their possible nonmembership in the wedding — the danger of their receiving a snub rather than an invitation to be bridesmaids—is past and they see nothing but tea and cakes from here on out. "But five of them were foolish *(mōraí)* and five were wise *(phrónimoi.)*"

Phrónimoi, of course, is the word used to describe the faithful and wise servant in the immediately preceding parable, so I am disposed to run with it in my interpretation. The foolish maidens represent the wisdom of this world — the live-by-what-you-see wisdom *(sophía)* that "God has made foolish *(emóranen:* 1 Cor. 1:20)." But the wise represent the wisdom of faith — the wisdom of trusting the foolishness of God in Christ crucified (1 Cor. 1:21-25) — the wisdom of living by the all-governing reality of the party to which the Bridegroom has invited all of creation. In actual fact, of course, both sets of girls have all they need for now, just as both the faithful and the unfaithful have identical shares of the world's goods or ills. But only the wise have the faith that will get them through their lives in solid contact with the presently unseeable and unknowable Bridegroom.

"For when the foolish took their lamps, they took no oil with them." The image is that of life lived on the ordinary, prudential basis of what is likely to happen. It is a picture of happy little winners assuming that their luck will always hold and that they need make no efforts to deal with the implausible. "But the wise took flasks of oil with their lamps." Notice how Jesus deliberately stands things on their heads. The five supposedly foolish girls, knowing that they have been invited to a daytime wedding that will last only into the early evening, reasonably assess their needs and content themselves with taking filled lanterns with them. Nothing could be more sensible. But the other five insist on dragging along bleach bottles full of kerosene, just in case. Nothing could be more idiotic: they have complicated their lives by preparing for an utterly unlikely contingency. Why does Jesus thus make the first group seem wiser than the second? He does it, I think, to preclude our interpreting the oil in the lamps as good works. The foolish girls are quite wise enough — quite sufficiently possessed of all the good works they will reasonably need for any wedding festivities the world may send their way. And the wise girls are not wise in any normal sense of the word; their possession of good works is portrayed as nothing less than neurotic: they are a bunch of belt-and-suspenders fussbudgets pre-occupied with what might possibly go wrong.

But the point of the story — the point that ultimately makes wisdom of their apparent folly—is that, in this world, something always does go wrong. And so in this parable, Jesus introduces just such a critical (from *krísis*) contretemps. "When the bridegroom took his time arriving *(chronízontos de tou nymphíou)*," he says, "they all slumbered and slept." The giggles go on through the day and into the evening. The lamps are lit and the ten maidens talk on into the night about which of their friends is pregnant by whom and how they would just die before they could ever confront their parents with a prob-lem like that. Finally, though, the wedding feast turns into a slumber party: all ten are sacked out on couches and across the floor.

"But at midnight there was a cry, 'Behold, the bridegroom! Come out to meet him!'" There are, I think, three things to note about this particular verse. First, it is a parable of the course of the world as it really is. The unexpected does hap-pen — regularly. As God brings the arrow of history to the bull's-eye, he does it very much in the style of the old joke about Jesus and Moses playing golf: by having it blown off course into the trees, bounced out into the rough, picked up by a passing hawk, and finally dropped on the target (con-veniently knocked over by the divine Fox himself) because the hawk just got tired of wasting his hunting time on arrows. The bridegroom's delayed arrival is a silly, gratuitous detail that can be justified only by one fact: it fits perfectly in a silly, gratu-itous world.

Second—and more darkly—this verse bears witness to the complicity of God not only in the slapstick way the world is run, but in the failures of those who counted on its being run in a more respectable fashion. For whose fault is it, ultimately, that the prudentially correct amount of oil in the foolish girls' lamps ran out? The bridegroom's, that's whose. And whose fault is it, finally, that Peter denied Jesus or that Judas betrayed him? It is God's. If God had left Peter in the fishing business,

Peter would never had gotten into waters he couldn't navigate. If God had left Judas to be just the smartest CPA in the county, Judas would never have been tempted to run Jesus' career for him. I said before that God is not an honest man. Well, he is not an innocent man either. He is just the only God we've got, and we're stuck with him. That he is also stuck with us—and stuck by us—may take the curse off it all; but it does not do a thing about his complicity in our failures. Why he couldn't have figured out a way of getting rid of sin without creating more sinners in the process is a big question. And the big answer is that there is no answer. No answer except Job's, "Though he slay me, yet will I trust him." No answer except Jesus', "Take this cup from me; nevertheless, not my will but yours be done."

There is, however, a third point to be made. "Behold, the bridegroom!" has become the church's watchword as it begins every Christian year with the season of Advent. That gives us a hint as to how we are to reconcile ourselves to both the slapstick of history and the complicity of God in evil. It is only as we wait in faith that all of the above ceases to matter and we are able to lay hold of the reconciliation that lies below the mess of history. Because if he finally does deliver on his promise to draw all to himself, if the reconciliation really is all ours no matter what our sins—if even Peter, even Judas, is within the drawing of his love and subject to the voice of his calling—then all we need is the faith to accept the reconciliation, no questions asked, from the hand of the one who brings it, no questions answered. Advent, therefore, is the church's annual celebration of the silliness (from *selig,* which is German for "blessed") of salvation. The whole thing really is a divine lark. God has fudged everything in our favor: without shame or fear we rejoice to behold his appearing. Yes, there is dirt under the divine Deliverer's fingernails. But no, it isn't any different from all the other dirt of history. The main thing is, he's got the package and we've got the trust: Lo, he comes with clouds descending. Alleluia, and three cheers.

But now Jesus brings on the *krisis* of unfaith, the judgment pronounced on those who thought that history could be brought home by something neater and more plausible than the mystery. "Then all those maidens rose and trimmed their lamps." They all take the ordinary, prudential steps that life in this world dictates as necessary. But then they discover something. All the wick trimming in the world—all the brilliant steps that might be taken to make a properly designed operation run right—are irrelevant. The operation is not properly designed. The bridegroom is late for his own party: God has taken so long to do anything that the world has dug its own grave in the meantime. Unless there is something other than the wisdom of the world to help it, there is nothing for the world to do but to lie down and die.

It is that something, therefore, that becomes the only matter of judgment in the parable. Now that all of the girls, wise or foolish, have found out there is no way of going on from here simply by going on from here, faith comes to the fore as the sole criterion for distinguishing between them. "And the foolish said to the wise, 'Give us some of your oil, for our lamps are going out.' But the wise replied, 'Perhaps there will not be enough for us and for you; go rather to the dealers and buy for yourselves.'" Time has at last run out, as it always does in real life. And since faith is at bottom something we do in real life, the time for faith has run out too. As I said, we should be slow to extrapolate from the parable and specify the historical or theological circumstances that might constitute such a dreadful expiration in our own or others' lives. But the parable does seem to say that since faith is a relationship with God, there will inevitably be a point at which he will say that the relationship does or does not exist. He will tell us whether we said yes or no. No one will get away with saying maybe forever.

I am aware that it is easy to object to the behavior Jesus assigns to the wise maidens. They are simply snotty. "There won't be enough for us if we give you some" is hardly an example of Christian sharing; furthermore, they know perfectly well that oil dealers go home at six, if not at four, in the afternoon. But if I have just gotten through urging you to accept a parcel from a Deliverer with grubby fingernails, I am not about to balk at bad manners from a Watchman trying to warn us there will be a time when our time will have run out. For that is the whole point of the parable: some day, late or soon, it will be too late even to believe. We become what we do. If we trust, we become trusters, and we enter into the sure possession of him whom we trust. If we distrust, we become distrusters and close out the only relationship with reality ever offered to us.

That closure is the note on which the parable ends. "While they went to buy, the bridegroom came, and those who were ready went in with him to the marriage feast; and the door was shut. Afterward the other maidens came also, saying, 'Lord, lord, open to us.' But he replied, 'Amen, I say to you, I do not know you.'" The shut door is God's final answer to the foolish wisdom of the world. In the death of Jesus, he closes forever the way of winning—the right-handed, prudential road to the kingdom, the path of living as the path of life. All the silly little girls with their Clorox bottles—all the neurotics of faith, all the wise fools who were willing to trust him in their lastness, lostness, leastness, and death—have gone into the party. And all the bright, savvy types who thought they had it figured are outside in the dark—with no oil and even less fun. The dreadful sentence, "Amen, I say to you, I never knew you," is simply the truth of their condition. He does not say, "I never called you." He does not say, "I never loved you." He does not say, "I never drew you to myself." He only says, "I never knew you—because you never bothered to know me."

Someone once said, "The world God loves is the world he sees in his only begotten Son." That fits here. For the world God sees in his only begotten Son consists of all those who have accepted their visibility in Jesus by faith. But those who have not accepted it, those who have pretended to make themselves invisible by their rejection of his acceptance of them, have the sentence of their self-chosen invisibility ratified by God. There was no relationship on their part; therefore God just says as much on his and gets on with the feast.

165

"Watch therefore," Jesus says at the end of the parable, "for you know neither the day nor the hour." When all is said and done—when we have scared ourselves silly with the now-or-never urgency of faith and the once-and-always finality of judgment—we need to take a deep breath and let it out with a laugh. Because what we are watching for is a party. And that party is not just down the street making up its mind when to come to us. It is already hiding in our basement, banging on our steam pipes, and laughing its way up our cellar stairs. The unknown day and hour of its finally bursting into the kitchen and roistering its way through the whole house is not dreadful; it is all part of the divine lark of grace. God is not our mother-in-law, coming to see whether her wedding-present china has been chipped. He is a funny Old Uncle with a salami under one arm and a bottle of wine under the other. We do indeed need to watch for him; but only because it would be such a pity to miss all the fun.

CHAPTER THIRTEEN

The End of the Storm (II)

The Talents; the Sheep and the Goats

The parable of the Talents (Aland no. 299; Matt. 25:14-30—the Matthean version of the parable of the Coins in Luke) has already been dealt with in chapter six of this book. I want to note here only how it picks up and enlarges upon some of the themes I have expounded in the parable of the Ten Virgins.

First, it is about a judgment rendered on faith-in-action, not on the results of that faith. Not only does the lord of the servants who doubled their talents praise them precisely as faithful ("well done, good and faithful [*pistós*] servant"); the doubling seems to be due more to the talents themselves than to the efforts the servants put into doing business with them. The servant who was given five makes five more; the one who received two makes two more. To me that says that the grace of acceptance does its own work; all we have to do is trust it. It emphatically does not say that God is a bookkeeper looking for productive results. The only bookkeeper in the parable is the servant who decided he had to fear a nonexistent audit and who therefore hid his one talent in the ground. And as if to underscore the indifference of God to bookkeeping, Jesus gives two twists to the parable. He has the lord say (to the useless servant) that he would have accepted anything—even rock-bottom savings-account interest—that the one talent might have produced as a result of faith-in-action. And he has the lord take the talent away from that servant and give it to the one who has ten. Were Jesus at pains to show that God was interested in bottom lines, why would he not have had the lord give it to the fellow with four? Why this bizarre enriching of the already rich, if not to show God's aversion to any counting at all? The goodness of his grace does all that needs doing. Here, therefore, as in the Laborers in the Vineyard, it is only the bookkeeping of unfaith that is condemned; the rest of the story is about the unaccountable, even irresponsible joy of the Lord who just wants everybody to be joyful with him.

That brings us to the second theme. As the parable of the Ten Virgins was about the happiness of the bridegroom at his wedding, so this one is about the ebullience of the lord's joy at throwing his money around. It is the theme of the divine party again, the party that lurks beneath the surface of history and calls only for a recognition by faith. It is the fatted calf served up for a prodigal who did nothing but come home in faith. It is the free champagne and caviar for wedding guests who did nothing but trust the king's insistence on providing fancy costumes and party hats. It is the full pay for next-to-no-work-at-all given to grape pickers who just said yes to a last-minute promise. The only reason that judgment comes into it at all is the sad fact that there will always be dummies who refuse to trust a good thing when it's handed to them on a platter. That is indeed a grim prospect. And it is grim because, if we have any knowledge of our own intractable stupidity, we know that those dummies could just as well be ourselves. But for all that, it is still about joy rather than fear. The final balance it strikes is the balance of Advent once again: without shame or fear we rejoice to behold his appearing because we have decided to believe him when he says he wills us nothing but the best.

And there is the third and last theme I want to underline: the sheer needlessness of fear, the utter nonnecessity of our ever having to dread God. The servant with his little shovel and his mousy apprehension that God is as small as himself is such a nerd! He is just one more of the pitiful turkeys that Jesus parades through his parables to shock us, if possible, into recognizing the stupidity of unfaith. The elder brother, the man without the wedding garment, the laborers who worked all day, the Pharisee who tried to wheedle God into thinking he was a good egg—all of these are cardboard figures, cartoon characters designed to elicit only a smile at the preposterousness of their behavior. It is also true, of course, that they are the figures we most easily identify with. But then that is because we are just as preposterous. We spend our lives invoking upon ourselves imagined necessities, creating God in the image of our own fears—and all the while, he is beating us over the head with the balloon of grace and the styrofoam baseball bat of a vindicating judgment. The history of salvation is slapstick all the way, right up to and including the end. It's the Three Stooges working only for laughs. God isn't trying to hurt anyone; he's not even mad at anyone. There are no lengths to which he won't go to prove there are no restrictions on the joy he wants to share with us. If you were never afraid of Curly, Larry, and Moe, you don't need to be afraid of the Trinity either.

Which makes a good enough introduction, I think, to the last of Jesus' parables, the story of the Great Judgment (Matt. 25:31-46; Aland no. 300). Because if it is in one way the heaviest, most fear-inspiring parable of all, it is also the lightest, the last laugh of the mighty act of salvation: it is the bestowal of the inheritance of the kingdom on a bunch of sheep who not only didn't know they were doing good works for God, but also never even knew they were faithful to him. And since no one who has heard this parable even once ever forgets it (I can still remember the Sunday afternoon in a Brooklyn church where I first heard it as a boy), I am not going to take you through it step by step. Instead, I shall try to set it in the context of Jesus' whole parabolic *oeuvre* (of which it is the grand finale) and to relate it to the general context of Scripture itself.

In the Great Judgment, all of the themes of Jesus' earlier parables come full circle. In the parables of the kingdom at the beginning of his ministry, he set forth a saving action of God that had five unique characteristics. He proclaimed a kingdom that was *catholic,* not parochial; that was *mysterious,* not recognizable; that was *actual,* not merely virtual or on the way; that was met with *hostility* as well as welcome; and that called for a *response of faith* rather than one of works. Now at the end we see those characteristics brought to fruition in a variety of ways.

The *catholicity* of the kingdom is *vindicated.* In this parable, it is precisely "*all* the nations" that are gathered together before the Son of man on his throne of glory. I am aware that the word "nations" (*éthnē,* the Gentiles) might tempt some to see this as an implicit exaltation of Gentiles over Jews, or even as bespeaking a rejection of the Jews. But since that requires attributing it more to the early church than to Jesus—and since I have pretty much stayed clear of Jew/Gentile interpretations in my treatment of the parables—I am not about to go in that direction at this late date. For one thing, Jesus was speaking to Jews: even though he clearly stigmatized the rejection of himself by the Jewish authorities, I do not think that any fair case can be made out for his excluding Jews as such from the operation of the kingdom—particularly since he first announced the catholicity of that operation to an exclusively Jewish audience. For another, though, the entire argument of Paul in the theological part of the epistle to the Romans is a progress toward verses 25-26 of chapter 11, in which he says specifically that "all Israel will be saved." Accordingly, I take the phrase "all nations" as referring to the whole world: the kingdom, which was first proclaimed as a catholic mystery, is now revealed as a catholic *fait accompli.* Not one scrap of creation, Jew or Gentile, good, bad, or indifferent, is left out of it. Jesus has literally drawn all to himself.

More than that, though, the catholicity of the kingdom is vindicated even with regard to goodness and badness: in the end as in the beginning, evil is not simply excluded but provided for—given a place in the final scheme of things. True enough, Jesus' parables of judgment are rife with images of separation: the outer darkness is the final destination of the man without the wedding garment and of the useless servant; the wrong side of the door is the portion of the foolish virgins. But in the Great Judgment, Jesus goes out of his way to stipulate that the Son of man "will separate them one from another *as a shepherd separates the sheep from the goats*." Do you see what that means? Jesus is the Good Shepherd, and the Good Shepherd lays down his life for the sheep. But he lays down his life for the goats as well, because on the cross he draws *all* to himself. It is not that the sheep are his but the goats are not; the sheep are his sheep and the goats are his goats. Any separation that occurs, therefore, must be read as occurring *within* his shepherding, not as constituting a divorce from it. (It was common in biblical times for a shepherd to keep both sheep and goats: see Gen. 30:32, for example; but see especially Exod. 12:5, where it is specified that even a goat can serve as the Paschal Lamb — "you shall take it from the sheep or from the goats.") Accordingly, Jesus' *drawing of all to himself* remains the ultimate gravitational force in the universe; nothing, not even evil, is ever exempted from it. Hell has no choice but to be within the power of the final party, even though it refuses to act as if it is at the party. It lies not so much outside the festivities as it is sequestered within them. It is hidden, if you will, in the spear wound in Christ's side to keep it from being a wet blanket on the heavenly proceedings; but it is not, for all that, any less a part of Jesus' catholic shepherding of his flock.

The *mystery* of the kingdom, to take up the next characteristic, is *revealed* at this final juncture. The iceberg of the divine presence under all of history at last thrusts itself up in one grand, never-to-be-hidden-again *parousía*. The Son of man has come in glory and everything is out in the open. All the waiting upon the mystery in faith is over and everyone, faithful or not, knows it. Time has not just run out; it has, like the fig tree, run its full course from winter's death to spring's new life: summer is now at hand. Not one bit of the operation of the kingdom will ever be hidden again, and all the previous sacraments of its working in the last, the lost, and the least are finally understood. Jesus has made all things, even the bad old things, new.

THE PARABLES OF JUDGMENT

As for the *actuality* of the kingdom — its real presence through the whole course of history—that note is *triumphant*. Since the kingdom cannot possibly become more present than it has been all along, this parable displays it as simply its own unchanged self, victorious. The kingdom prepared from the foundation of the world—the whole mysterious inheritance that has always been available to faith—now publicly dazzles its inheritors with a knowable, palpable beauty. Jesus has had a party going from the first day in Genesis; now, at the Marriage Supper of the Lamb, he drinks a toast to the fact that it will never end.

That leaves just two further characteristics of the kingdom —*hostility* and *response*—for this parable to fulfill; and since I am going to read it as relating both of them to faith, I shall deal with the two simultaneously. On the one hand, the hostility with which the kingdom was met throughout history was never portrayed by Jesus as anything other than *unfaith;* on the other, the response called for by the kingdom was never stipulated as anything but *faith*. This is particularly important because of the facility with which interpreters of this parable slip into moralistic expositions. It is so easy to make the cursed goats at the King's left hand into bad people loaded down with sins of omission; and it is even easier to make the blessed sheep at his right hand into do-gooders. But that simply will not bear the light of comparison with the rest of Jesus' teaching. We need to remind ourselves again that he habitually avoids depicting badness as an obstacle to the kingdom, just as he carefully steers clear of making goodness one of its entrance requirements. In the parables of grace, for example, he displays unreformed bad people (the prodigal, the publican) as acceptable by faith rather than by works; and in the parables of the kingdom, he goes out of his way to show both good and evil as existing side by side *within the kingdom:* in the Wheat and the Weeds, he lets both grow together until the harvest; in the Net, he says that the kingdom gathers every kind. True enough, he says that at the consummation there will be a separation of the good from the bad—and in this parable, admittedly, he says much the same thing. I have, however, two observations to make about all that.

The first is an extension of what I said above about Jesus being the Shepherd of both the sheep and the goats. The separation of the two is a disposition made by the Good Shepherd himself in the interests of his own goodness, not in regard to some supposed inability on his part to put up with evil. It is a provision by the King for the best possible government of all the subjects of his kingship. At least in some sense, therefore, the separation remains within the flock and within the kingdom. The Shepherd/King does not have a problem with evil: Jesus has taken all the evil of the world into himself. The final dispensation is not a destruction of evil; it is precisely a sequestration of evil in the Son of God. Accordingly, whatever else hell may be, it is not where God isn't: if it exists at all, it exists because he, in his creating Word, is intimately and immediately present to it. Jesus is the Life even of those who go down into the second death; he is the shepherd even of the goats whom he divides from his sheep. Accordingly, on this point I want simply to run up a flag: the separation imagery of the parables is a tricky piece of business; for my money, it should not be interpreted in a way that portrays Jesus as having taken off the velvet glove of grace and put on brass knuckles. Above all, it should not be read in this parable as turning the Good Shepherd into the wolf.

My other observation goes to the centrality of faith as the criterion of the separation. As I have said, throughout the whole body of his parables, Jesus spends a great deal of time denying that goodness or badness has anything to do with salvation. The gift of grace, as he portrays it, is a gift of acceptance already granted—a gift that it takes only a response of trust to enjoy. The prodigal is not portrayed as cleaning up his life, only as accepting his father's acceptance. The eleventh-hour laborers are not shown as having earned their pay by twelvefold exertions, only as having trusted the vineyard owner. And the publican is not sent home justified because he said he would lead a better life, only because he had the faith to confess his death and to trust in a God who could raise the dead. Accordingly, as far as this parable is concerned, I am not about to come to it prepared to hear Jesus say that he wasted his time establishing faith rather than goodness as the means of appropriating the gift of salvation. And therefore I am not about to interpret Jesus' attitude here as a new tack either on hostility against the kingdom or on response to it.

What do I say then about the note of hostility as it appears in this parable? The same thing I said about it when it appeared in the earlier parables: it was aced out in them; it is likewise aced out in this. Evil is not so much banished as provided for—and provided for in a way that draws its fangs. Its existence is not withdrawn but contained within the divine *áphesis,* the ultimately gracious dispensation of God's forgiveness. As the master of the house in the parable of the Wheat and the Weeds does the least damaging thing he can think of with the weeds ("Let [*áphete*] both grow together until the harvest"), so the King in this parable does the least damaging thing he can think of with the cursed ("You never did like my parties. Why don't you just go downstairs to do your sulking?"). To be sure, the language with which he issues that final invitation to get out is severe (everlasting fire prepared for the devil and his angels, eternal punishment); and since I am admittedly seeking a more graceful interpretation, my first temptation is to label it Oriental hyperbole and let it go at that. But on second thought, the language, hyperbolic or not, is not without a built-in reference to grace: it is of a piece, in fact, with the note of grace that Jesus often sounds when he broaches the theme of judgment in his parables. For while this parable is judgmental in the extreme, it cannot possibly come as a surprise since in a number of other parables the original catholic invitation to come into the party was itself a judgment, a *krísis* on the whole world that received it. In the parable of the King's Son's Wedding, for example, the *krísis* of the invitation falls upon the guests that reject it in the form of battle, murder, and sudden death. And why? Well, not because they had done unworthy things; as a matter of fact, the invitation itself had made them worthy from the start. No, the real reason it fell on them was because they did not trust the King's proclamation of their worthiness—because, in a word, they did not believe. And while such mayhem is indeed a dramatic way of showing how God chooses to throw a party, it is not one bit too dramatic for showing how terribly serious he is about his plans for the eternal season. For as the party in the Prodigal Son cost the fatted calf its life, so this party cost the King his life. He is not about to write it all off as a whim.

All of which tips my hand quite sufficiently as to what I have to say about the note of response to the kingdom. The response called for all through the parables is faith, not good works; therefore the response called for here at the end is the same. As the oil in the wise virgins' vessels should not be interpreted as quarts and quarts of ethical integrity, so the kindnesses of the blessed to the least of the King's brethren should not be taken as drumsful of industrial-strength good deeds. Indeed, the most notable feature of the parable of the Great Judgment is that the good works of the blessed are not presented as such. The King says not that the sheep have compiled a splendid moral record, but that they had a relationship with himself: "Amen, I say to you, inasmuch as you did it to one of the least of these my brethren, you did it to *me*." Or to put it even more precisely, they are praised at his final *parousía* for what they did in his *parousía* throughout their lives, namely, for trusting *him* to have had a relationship with them all along.

And what, finally, of the cursed whose response of unfaith —whose refusal to relate to him in the lost and the least—receives the King's condemnation? Well, I think we must be careful here. I have already issued two warnings against defining too narrowly the precise circumstances that will constitute grounds for such a sentence. I want now to issue a caveat against defining them at all. Jesus came to raise the dead, not to reform the reformable, and certainly not to specify the degree of nonreform that will nullify the sovereign grace of resurrection. He came to proclaim a kingdom that works only in the last, the lost, the least, and the little, not to set up a height-weight chart for the occupants of the heavenly Jerusalem. And while we may think we might do well to supply the ethico-theological requirements he has so carefully omitted—while we may be just itching to define what constitutes rejection of him at the hour of death or relationship with him in the underdogs of the world—we are wrong on both counts. In the first place, we don't know enough about anybody, not even ourselves, to say anything for sure. But in the second, Jesus shows us in this parable that even those who did relate to him didn't know what they were doing. "Come, you blessed of my Father," the King says to those on his right hand, "and inherit the kingdom . . . for I was hungry and you fed me, I was thirsty and you gave me drink, I was a stranger and you welcomed me. . . ." And the righteous answer and say to him, "Uhh . . . pardon us, Your Highness, but when was that?"

Do you finally see? Nobody *knows* anything. The righteous didn't know they were in relationship with the King when they ministered to the least of his brethren, any more than the cursed knew they were despising the King when they didn't so minister. Knowledge is not the basis of anybody's salvation or damnation. Action-in-dumb-trust is. And the reason for that is that salvation comes only by relationship with the Savior—by a relationship that, from his side, is already an accomplished eternal fact, and that therefore needs only to be *accepted by faith,* not known in any way. "No man," Luther said (if I may quote him one last time), "can know or feel he is saved; he can only believe it." At the final *parousía,* we will not be judged by anything except our response of faith or unfaith to the Savior whose presence was coterminous with our whole existence. And at that day he will simply say whether, from our side (by faith, that is—but with no other conditions specified as to knowledge or any other human achievement), we related to that presence. He will simply *do the truth* from his side—simply affirm his eternal, gracious relationship with all of creation—and honor what both the sheep and the goats did with that truth from their side.

It is John 3:16ff. all over again. The Gospel truth is, "God so loved the world that he gave his only begotten Son, that everyone who believes in him should not perish but have ever-lasting life." And that truth *as it vindicates us* is, "The one who believes in him is not judged: but the one who does not believe has been judged already because he has not believed in the name of the only begotten Son of God." But that truth *as we are to respond to it in our lives* is not at all a matter of our intel-lectual scrutiny. From our side, we can only respond to it by "doing the truth" ourselves, that is, by admitting our death and "coming to the light," that it may be made manifest that our deeds—all of them, good or bad—were done in the God who makes all things new.

What counts, therefore, is not what we know (most of that can only count against us) but what *he* knows. And what he knows is that "God did not send his Son into the world to judge the world, but that the world might be saved by him." His saving relationship with the world has already been estab-lished—and it will stay established forever. The only question at the end is whether we trusted the truth of it and made it a two-sided relationship, or whether we distrusted it and left it a relationship from his side only. And Jesus alone knows the answer to that question. In this last parable of all, he delib-erately deprives us of any way of even thinking about it: the only ground the Great Judgment gives us for hope is *trust in his presence in the passion of the world*. But since no one will ever quite manage to be apart from that passion—since we do not need to stipulate anyone's participation in it—this parable also deprives us of the luxury of telling the world all the compli-cated things it has to do to get on the right side of his eschato-logical presence. The only thing we can possibly do is give the world the living witness of our trust in his presence in its pas-sion. We need only to act as if we really believe he meets us in leastness and death. The rest is his business, not ours.

And therefore all the theological baggage about repen-tances that come too late or acts of faith that peak too soon, all the fine slicing about how maybe a suicide who has time to think between the bridge and the river is in better shape than one who blew his brains out—and all the doctrinal jury-rigging designed to give the unbaptized a break or to prove that unbelievers are invincibly ignorant—all of it is idle, mischievous, and dead wrong. We simply don't know, and we should all have the decency to shut up and just trust him in the passion we cannot avoid. And we don't even have to know if we have succeeded in doing that, because Jesus is there anyway and he is on everybody's side. He is the Love that will not let us go. If anybody can sort it all out, he can; if he can't, nobody else ever will. Trust him, therefore. And trust him now.

There is nothing more to do.

CHAPTER FOURTEEN

Epilogue

It is all bizarre. At the end of his parables, Jesus goes ahead and acts out what he has been talking about from the beginning. In his passion, death, resurrection, and ascension he manifests in his own person the nontransactional mystery of a kingdom that has always disposed all things mightily and sweetly by grace. But even in those fulfilling, mighty acts, the mystery remains nontransactional. They are not discrete pieces of business that the world is expected to enter into a cooperative relationship with. They are rather sacraments, acted parables of a relationship established from the foundation of the world. They are invitations to trust the passion, the *inaction*, of the Incarnate Word of God in whom all things are already made new.

And that is bizarre because just as in the spoken parables nothing much is tidied up in the temporal order of things— just as the lastness, lostness, leastness, and death of Jesus' parabolic characters are shown not as inconveniences they are saved from but as disasters they are saved in—so in these culminating, acted parables. Neither Jesus' death, nor his resurrection, nor his ascension makes the least practical difference in the way the world now runs. We still die, even though we believe sin has been overcome by grace; and we are still nobodies, even though we believe we are heirs of the kingdom.

It is not an easy Gospel to proclaim: it looks for all the

world as if we are not only trying to sell a pig in a poke, but an invisible pig at that. The temptation, of course, is by hook or by crook to produce a visible pig for the world's inspection— to prove that trust in Jesus heals the sick, spares the endangered, fattens the wallet, or finds the lost keys. But it does not. And it does not because the work of Jesus is not a transaction—not a repair job on the world as it now is, but an invitation of the world as it now is into the death out of which it rises only in him. The only honest way to advertise the Gospel, therefore, is to admit that it proclaims two orders at once, the old and the new—and to confine our promotional efforts to the insistence that faith is the human race's only dependable way of breaking through from the first to the second.

I realize you can quote me a dozen passages to prove otherwise—to prove that Jesus or Peter or Paul spoke on occasion as if we ourselves were somehow responsible for making the kingdom happen in this world, for building Jerusalem in England's green and pleasant land. But I am still not persuaded. "The kingdom of God does not come in such a way as to be seen" (Luke 17:20). The only sure evidence of the kingdom we have ever seen is Jesus, and he died just as dead as any of us. To be sure, he also rose; but then he left, leaving us only with his mysterious presence in the world's passion as the meeting point of the two orders. The pig or, better said, the Lamb in the poke disappears, leaving us holding only the bag, in faith.

That may sound depressing, but it is not. And it is not depressing precisely because the bag we hold—the crumpled and tattered sack of history—is the grandest of all the sacraments of his presence. It is the one place, both now and at the end, where we are invited to believe we will find him. We are not told that he expects us to iron the bag smooth before he will come and dwell in it; we are told, in his parables and on the cross, that he is in it already by the power of his death and resurrection. And therefore when the church tries to iron the bag —when it implies that its primary mission is to make history smooth here and now—it fails both its Lord and the world.

It fails its Lord, because it is trying to do something Jesus in the end neither said nor did; and it fails the world, because it is offering it a false hope. Neither history nor revelation encourages the least expectation that plugging in anyone's iron —even God's—is going to turn the world back into Eden. What we are really invited to believe is that there is a New Jerusalem waiting to come down and marry the Lamb who was in the bag all along. If you reduce the promise of the Gospel to anything less bizarre than that, you simply turn the leap of faith into a mere standing on tiptoes to see something that isn't going to happen.

But if you aggravate the bizarreness of the promise—if you take your stand on salvation by grace, on salvation through faith, on salvation in the very shipwreck of history—all the lights go on. Not only do you have the only unassailable apologetic there is (you need never ask anyone to believe anything other than what is, only to trust Jesus in it all); you also have the joy of being in on the divine mirth. For the promise is wild beyond all imagining. It is the gift of life in the midst of death, of a Way out simply by remaining in, of everything for nothing. It is the promise that the God who has been with us all along in the old world will be with us forever in the new. "Behold, the tent of God is with men and he will dwell among them and they will be his people and God himself will be with them and be their God. And he will wipe away every tear from their eyes and death will be no more, neither will there be mourning nor crying nor pain any more, for the former things have passed away" (Rev. 21:3-4).

Trust him, therefore. There really is nothing more to do.